SATAN'S KINGDOM AND THE SECOND COMING

Published by

SOUTHWEST RADIO CHURCH
P.O. Box 1144
Oklahoma City, Oklahoma 73101

1 copy for $5.00 offering; 3 copies for $10.00 offering
10 copies for $25.00 offering; $1.50 in lots of 25 or more.

Rev. Noah Hutchings has devoted himself to full-time Christian service since his profession of faith in the Lord Jesus Christ. Pastor Hutchings was born on December 11, 1922, in Hugo, Oklahoma. After World War II, he returned to school and obtained a degree in accounting and business administration. While waiting for a position with a large industrial firm, he answered an ad for part-time work. The part-time work was with the radio evangelist, Dr. E.F. Webber. Noah was saved through faith in Christ, and when the position with the large company opened up, he chose rather to remain in God's service. For the past 27 years Rev. Hutchings has been active in doing research and writing for daily Gospel radio programs. He has also served as office manager of The Southwest Radio Church, and spoken on specific topics in the light of biblical truth, and on prophetic subjects, in various meetings throughout the nation. He is editor of the Gospel Truth, a publication of the radio ministry which is read and reproduced in the United States and in several countries.

TABLE OF CONTENTS

Chapter   **Page**

The Unseen World

There is an unseen world: a world our hands cannot touch, our eyes cannot see, our ears cannot hear. In this unseen world a battle is raging – a battle between God and Satan. Though we cannot see this world or its combatants, they are there just the same. The agents of the devil today are some of the best-educated men and women who are even leaders of their own professions. The late Bishop James Pike was recognized as a leading theologian in championing the modernistic doctrines, yet he was convinced that he talked with his dead son through a spirit being.

In practically all nations today, illiteracy is being abolished. Almost every child receives a high-school education, and an increasingly larger percentage go to college. But never has there been such a revival in spiritism and Satanism. It is no longer illogical to believe in witches and evil spirits. These are popular subjects to explore.

God said that in these last days the devil would flood the world with fallen angels and demons. According to Revelation 12:9, the day is coming when the devil himself and all his hordes will be cast out from Heaven forever and confined to this Earth, and by the increase of spirit activity, we know that this day spoken of by God is near at hand.

Some may be reticent to accept the proposition presented in the Scriptures and embraced by millions today, that there is a personal devil and there are spirit beings traversing the heavens and invading the Earth. But God Himself declares it. I Corinthians 15:39, 40 says: *"All flesh is not the same flesh: but there is one kind of flesh of men, another flesh of beasts, another of fishes, and another of birds. There are also celestial bodies, and bodies terrestrial: but the glory of the celestial is one, and the glory of the terrestrial is another."*

First, the Scriptures divide terrestrial life into four main divisions: men, beasts, fishes, and birds. God created each of these four divisions with a body to function and operate within the environment in which it was placed. If men had never seen a bird, they would scoff at the idea that there existed a form of animal life that could fly in the air. If men had never seen or heard of a fish, they would find it difficult to believe a form of animal life could live by breathing under water, or that this species could be frozen and then brought back to life.

The apostle Paul went one step further to declare that apart from the four main divisions of terrestrial life, there was celestial life. The Word of God further declares that this celestial life was created to operate and function within all the environments found throughout the universe. Therefore, these spirit beings have bodies that will endure the extremely cold temperatures that exist in outer space.

They also probably must live in places where there is no oxygen; and according to the biblical description, they must travel at speeds approaching or exceeding the speed of light. There is no known life form on Earth that can exist in such environments; yet we know from the Bible that such celestial beings are in existence, and the spirit activity in evidence today indicates that they are also here on Earth.

There is but a thin veil between the spirit world and the world of the natural man. Spirits desire to possess the bodies of men, and some men and women seek after spiritual contact with the powers of the air. Often the dimension of the spirit and the dimension of the flesh merge and become visible to each other. Abraham talked with the angels who visited him, and their bodies looked like those of men (Genesis 18). Daniel conversed freely with Gabriel (Daniel 8,9). The night that Christ was born, the shepherds near Bethlehem saw a multitude of the heavenly host (Luke 2:8-20).

The heavenly hosts faithful to God are made up of Seraphim (God's watchers over the creation – Daniel 4); Cherubim (the guardians of the third heaven – Genesis 3:24); the angels (God's faithful servants and messengers throughout the cosmos – Psalm 68:17, Isaiah 66:15); and the Archangels (God's princes who rule over the angels – Jude 9, Daniel 12:1).

As far as we know, there were never more than three archangels. Although Michael is the only archangel identified as such in the Bible, most theologians agree that Scripture indicates there are two others, Gabriel and Lucifer. However, Lucifer fell from his exalted position when iniquity was found in him. It may be concluded from scriptural information available that each archangel ruled over one-third of the angelic host. Revelation 12:3,4 seems to lend validity to this interpretation, *"And there appeared another wonder in heaven; and behold a great red dragon... And his tail drew the third part of the stars of heaven..."*

The great red dragon is identified in Revelation 12:9 as Satan, and stars are often used in the Bible as symbolic of angels. Thus, it becomes evident as we search the Scriptures that Satan, when he was the bright and shining one named Lucifer, ruled over one-third of the heavenly bodies and he had under his dominion one-third of the angelic hosts.

We read in Isaiah 14:12 that Lucifer was called the "son of the morning," indicating that he was one of the first to be created. In Ezekiel 28:12 he is said to have been full of wisdom and perfect in beauty. In Ezekiel 28:13-17 we discover further that he was full of brightness. The name *Lucifer* in the Hebrew means "the bright and shining one." But, as we find also in Ezekiel 28 and Isaiah 14, because of his exalted position he became vain and proud. He sought to exalt his own throne above all the stars of God, the angelic host. He knowingly and consciously rebelled against God. He was the first sinner, the first rebel, the first apostate. Instead of "the wise one," he became a liar and a murderer. Instead of the son of the morning, he became the devil, our adversary. Instead of the bright and shining one, he became the serpent, that old dragon, the king of the demons, the prince of darkness.

Satan used his great wisdom to lie and deceive the angels under his dominion. They followed him in his rebellion against God to conquer the universe. He is still using his perverted wisdom and wickedness to deceive the world today. The fallen angels, his loyal subjects, are invading Earth to prepare the way for Satan's false Messiah, the Antichrist. This appears to be the reason for the alarming rise in spiritism, witchcraft, and Satanism. It is a sign that we are living in the terminal generation. Satanic activity is a sign that the time of sorrows, known as the Tribulation period, is about to break upon the world.

The intensity of spirit activity in the last days is described in Revelation 16:13,14: *"And I saw three unclean spirits like frogs come out of the mouth of the dragon, and out of the mouth of the beast, and out of the mouth of the false prophet. For they are the spirits of the devils, working miracles, which go forth unto the kings of the earth and of the whole world, to gather them to the battle of that great day of God Almighty."*

This is John's description of demons spreading over the face of the Earth; we are living at the time of the beginning of this spirit activity today. The final battle of this age between the forces of Satan and the forces of God is described in Revelation 12:7,8, *"And there was war in heaven: Michael and his angels fought against the dragons: and the dragon fought and his angels, And prevailed not; neither was their place found any more in heaven."*

John saw, by revelation, the final and deciding battle, but the war began millennia ago when Satan declared in his heart: *". . . I will ascend into heaven, I will exalt my throne above the stars of God: I will sit also upon the mount of the congregation, in the sides of the north: I will ascend above the heights of the clouds; I will be like the most High"* (Isaiah 14:13,14).

Being born again into the Kingdom of God, Christians are active participants in the spiritual war between God and the devil. Paul wrote in Ephesians 6:10-12, *"Finally, my brethren, be strong in the Lord, and in the power of his might. Put on the whole armour of God, that ye may be able to stand against the wiles of the devil. For we wrestle not against flesh and blood, but against principalities, against powers, against the rulers of the darkness of this world, against spiritual wickedness in high places."*

The rapid spread of Satan worship was noted in the August 16, 1971 edition of *Newsweek*, which stated in part: *"What democracies in general, and America in particular, most lack is belief in the Devil,' argued Denis deRougemont a quarter century ago. But if few Americans outside the Bible Belt were willing then to give the devil his due, today tens of thousands across the U.S. — some of them middle-class adults with advanced university degrees — are dabbling in Satanism, witchcraft, voodoo, and other forms of black or white magic . . . a good deal of the experimentation results from plain blind faith in Satanic power, which sometimes produces macabre acts of violence and sex . . . "*

This news article related specific crimes of murder and sex mutilation so horrible that we are reticent to offend our readers with descriptions of them. The article continued, *"... most of those convicted or suspected of such killings have demonstrated some kind of involvement with the Church of Satan."*

In the past decade, crimes associated with Satan worshippers have increased. The August 2, 1979 edition of *The Santa Monica Evening Outlook,* in an article on Satan worship, reported in part, *"Bobby Joe Maxwell, the alleged 'Skid Roe Stabber,' said he belongs to a cult that worships the devil and slew 11 derelicts in downtown Los Angeles to get 'souls for Satan,' court documents allege... Guards and inmates at Fort Pillow State Prison in Tennessee, where Maxwell served two years for robbery, said Maxwell conducted satanic rituals in his cell and tried to convert other inmates to his beliefs... the words 'satan power' and 'praise be unto the father of the prince of darkness' were found in a ledger kept by Maxwell."*

The Scriptures contend that there are many "wiles" of the devil; the growing power of Satan in the world manifests itself in many forms. The August 6, 1979 edition of *Time* reported on the increasing number of witches and participants in occult worship in the world: *"As 250 fellow worshipers formed a circle around them and chanted the ancient Hindu mantra 'om,' the bride and bridegroom watched the priest and priestess and their helpers conjure into their midst the gods and goddesses of the four elements — air, water, earth and fire... The bizarre ceremony, performed in a scruffy campground outside Demotte, Ind., was not some stunt but a modern pagan 'handfasting,' or wedding. It was one of the highlights of the Third Annual Pan Pagan Festival, a four-day conclave that brought together a witches brew of 325 paganists, occultists and witches from 26 states and Canada... The festival, organized by a group called the Midwest Pagan Council, reflected what some religious leaders find to have been a rather rapid spread of neo-paganism around the country over the past decade. J. Gordon Melton, an Evanston, Ill., Methodist minister who heads the Institute for the Study of American Religion, reckons that there may be as many as 4,000 practicing pagans today.*

According to reports, occult groups are massing and forming colonies across the world. In the United States such organizations are buying property and even in some instances, incorporating as cities or townships, or taking over existing cities and townships. One of the most noted of these is located in Antelope, Oregon. The July 4, 1982 edition of the *Sunday Oregonian* reported: *"About 6,000 followers of Bhagwan Shree Rajneesh were joined by their spiritual teacher... as a five-day festival began about 20 miles southeast of Antelope. The festival coincides with the first anniversary of the Rajneesh Foundation International's purchase of the 64,000-acre Muddy Ranch. It also is a celebration of Guru Purima, the traditional Eastern observance in which devotees gather with their masters... To accomodate the red-clad visitors attracted to the festival, three tent cities — close to 2,000 tents in all — have been set up on the ranch. The compounds, named for Buddha, Socrates and Zarathustra... The tent dwellers... come from across the globe. Australians, Germans, Brazilians and many other nationalities are represented in the throngs that line the country road each afternoon as Rajneesh takes his daily spin in one of his Rolls-Royces."*

According to various newspaper reports regarding this movement, wives are leaving their children and husbands, and husbands are deserting their mates, to live in this commune type of free love society. The head of the movement, Rajneesh, projects a father-God figure to his followers, a savior who promises love, peace and relief from all responsibilities and stress. He is just one of the thousands of false christs appearing on the world scene today. Even schools, churches and so-called youth rehabilitation agencies are using occult meditation practices to open the minds of young people to demonic possession. Jesus said of the end of the age: *"For many shall come in my name, saying, I am Christ; and shall deceive many"* (Matthew 24:5).

Satan is making his final effort to forever annex Earth to his kingdom. This battle, and life-and-death struggle during the coming Tribulation, will determine the future of the heavens and the Earth. We know the outcome from God's Word, but the beginning of the struggle signifies a time of great tribulation ahead. Christians should put on the whole armor of God so that they may stand against the wiles of the devil (Ephesians 6:13-18).

Spirit Activity In The Heavens

The Scriptures are replete with references concerning the teeming activities of the spirit world in the heavens. We read in Hebrews 12:22 that the angels who inhabit heavenly places are innumerable. All angels are not of the same order. In Scripture we read of Seraphim, Cherubim, Angels (some serving God and some serving the devil), Archangels, Principalities, Powers, Thrones, Dominions, Fallen Angels, Spirits in Prison, Demons, Seducing Spirits, Sons of God, Morning Stars, Watchers and Elders.

Perhaps the most complete picture of the relationship of the spirit world to the throne of God is found in the fourth chapter of Revelation. During the course of the Revelation of Jesus Christ, John was caught up into the presence of God, and he saw the throne of God. There is a literal Kingdom of God, and like every kingdom, God's Kingdom has a throne.

Revelation 4: 4,6-8 says: *"And round about the throne were four and twenty seats: and upon the seats I saw four and twenty elders sitting, clothed in white raiment; and they had on their heads crowns of gold . . . And before the throne there was a sea of glass like unto crystal: and in the midst of the throne, and round about the throne, were four beasts full of eyes before and behind. And the first beast was like a lion, and the second beast like a calf, and the third beast had a face as a man, and the fourth beast was like a flying eagle. And the four beasts had each of them six wings about him; and they were full of eyes within: and they rest not day and night, saying, Holy, holy, holy, Lord God Almighty, which was, and is, and is to come."*

The scene which John describes around the throne of God depicts the higher echelons of God's governmental administration. The king of any monarchal type of government is always the center of supreme authority. From the king, authority in administrative rule is delegated to cabinet members, prime ministers, judges, and so on. The four angelic creatures before the throne of God are called beasts because they have the appearance of certain beasts in the animal kingdom. The root word in the Greek text for beasts in this Scripture is *zoon*, indicating that the English translators were correct in their interpretation. These beasts rest neither day nor night. They are full of eyes, indicating they are ever watching.

The 24 elders are upon the seats. The word "seat" is still used to refer to delegated and administrative governmental authority, as when politicians "run for a seat" in Congress.

The four watchers, by their very nature, indicate that they watch over the whole creation, including lower life forms. This is also substantiated by Revelation 4:11: *" . . . for thou hast created all things, and for thy pleasure they are and were created."*

The fourth chapter of Daniel affords some light into the administrative duties of the elders, also called holy ones, and the watchers. We read in verses 13,16,17: *"I saw in the visions of my head upon my bed, and, behold, a watcher and an holy one came down from heaven . . . Let his* (meaning Nebuchadnezzar's) *heart be changed from man's, and let a beast's heart be given unto him; and let seven times pass over him. This matter is by the decree of the watchers, and the demand by the word of the holy ones: to the intent that the living may know that the most High ruleth in the kingdom of men, and giveth it to whomsoever he will, and setteth up over it the basest of men."*

One of the watchers, one of the four beasts, gave Nebuchadnezzar a beast's heart: the king ate straw in the field like an ox. The holy ones demanded that Nebuchadnezzar's kingdom be taken from him, and the watchers fulfilled the decree. Some interpret the 24 elders around the throne of God to be saints, but this view is without Scriptural foundation. It is apparent that the elders are of a higher angelic order. They are shown to work in conjunction with the watchers in Daniel, and we must also apply the same rule of interpretation to Revelation 4.

In addition to the elders and the watchers, there are elite angelic guardian forces of God called cherubim. In Genesis 3:24, we read that God placed cherubim around the Garden of Eden to keep man from eating of the "tree of life" and living forever in a godless and lost condition. Cherubim were placed over the mercy seat, indicating their protective position around the throne of God.

Another rank of the angelic order is the seraphim. We read of them in Isaiah 6:6,7: *"Then flew one of the seraphims unto me, having a live coal in his hand, which he had taken with the tongs from the altar. And he laid it upon my mouth, and said, Lo, this hath touched thy lips; and thine iniquity is taken away, and thy sin is purged."*

The root word for *seraphim* means "serpent." They have six wings, like the watchers before God's throne, but their role in God's government appears to be more of a priestly nature. They have charge over the altar of God in Heaven from which the burning coal came to take away the iniquity of Isaiah.

Another order of the spirit world is the angels. Angels are messengers and servants of God who serve throughout the universe, and they are so great in number that they cannot be counted. There is nothing said in Scripture about angels having wings. Their celestial travel is associated with the chariots of God. We read in Psalm 68:17 that *"The chariots of God are twenty thousand, even thousands of angels . . . "* Isaiah 66:15 says: *"For, behold, the Lord will come with fire, and with his chariots like a whirlwind, to render his anger with fury, and his rebuke with flames of fire."* Angels are described in appearance as looking like men; the Bible tells us that men are a little lower than the angels. Angels eat food. We know this because Abraham served the angels who visited him a hearty meal. We read in Psalm 78:24,25: *"And . . . rained down manna upon them to eat, and had given them of the corn of heaven. Man did eat angels' food . . . "*

The last identifiable members of the angelic order are the archangels, possibly the most important and trusted members of God's Kingdom. They are the only ones of God's angels mentioned by name. Since the fall of Lucifer, there are only two of these, and their names are Gabriel and Michael. We read in Jude 9: *". . . Michael the archangel, when contending with the devil he disputed about the body of Moses . . . "* Gabriel is mentioned by name in Daniel 8:16 and other Scriptures, and in Daniel 12:1 the archangels are called princes. Michael is called a prince of God, and therefore it follows that Gabriel is also a prince. The identification of the archangels as princes gives them throne rights in the Kingdom of God, and the Word indicates that Gabriel and Michael each rule over one-third of God's Kingdom and each commands one-third of the angelic host. This completes the roster of the spirit world within the universe who are faithful to God.

Next, let us identify the members of the spirit world who are in rebellion against God. At the head of the "Kingdom of Darkness" is Lucifer, who became Satan and the devil. We know from Scripture that God did not create a devil, but that one of the exalted ones of God's Kingdom became ambitious and because of pride, determined to elevate his throne above the throne of God. We read in Isaiah 14:12,13: *"How art thou fallen from heaven, O Lucifer, son of the morning! how art thou cut down to the ground, which didst weaken the nations? For thou hast said in thine heart, I will ascend into heaven, I will exalt my throne above the stars of God: I will sit also upon the mount of the congregation, in the sides of the north."* We read in verse 14 that Lucifer said in his heart that he would become like God.

How did Lucifer conceive such an ambition? What prompted it? In order to understand what changed this angelic being from a faithful servant of God into a prince of evil and darkness (the god of this world), we must go back to the dawn of creation.

We know the angels, like man, were a direct creation of God (Heb. 1:6). However, nothing is said of their creation within the six days of creation in Genesis 1. Their creation must date back to the dawn of creation mentioned in Genesis 1:1: *"In the beginning God created the heaven and the earth."* Angels are called the "sons of God," because they were created beings. They do not reproduce or have the power to reproduce themselves. Originally, it would appear that the spirit world fell into two categories – the sons of God (the angels), and the first created, "the morning stars." Both orders were created prior to the creation of the world. We read in Job 38:4,7: *"Where wast thou when I laid the foundations of the earth . . . When the morning stars sang together, and all the sons of God shouted for joy?"*

Let us keep in mind, as we trace the tragic career of Satan, that God rewards faithful service. To the redeemed from the human race, God has promised that some will sit on thrones, some will judge, and some will sit in heavenly places with Christ; there are many rewards and degrees of authority and responsibility to be determined at the Judgment Seat of Christ. If this be true of the future estate of the saved from among men, and indeed it is true, then it follows that the same rule of rewards for service could also apply to the angels.

From the higher angelic order which was created in the beginning, the morning stars, it appears that many were selected to fill positions of leadership in God's Kingdom. Let us now follow the career of one particular member of this angelic order, the one who eventually became Satan, our adversary.

1. Lucifer was originally a "son of the morning" (Isaiah 14:12).

2. He advanced to the status of a trusted cherubim, a member of the heavenly guard. We read in Ezekiel 28:14: *"Thou are the anointed cherub that covereth; and I have set thee so . . . "*

3. From the status of a cherubim, a position which he must have filled most admirably, he advanced to the status of a seraphim, a priest in the temple of God in Heaven. We read in Ezekiel 28:14: *". . . thou wast upon the holy mountain of God; thou hast walked up and down in the midst of the stones of fire."*

4. Probably the next promotion that Lucifer received was an appointment to be a watcher before the throne of God. Because of the similarity in appearance, a watcher is apparently a higher order of seraphim. Of the four watchers described in Revelation 4:7, one has the face of a lion, a watcher over the wild animal kingdom; one has the face of a man, a watcher over the human race; and one has the face of an eagle, a watcher over the bird kingdom. We notice that there is no watcher over the reptiles, and the reason is given in Habakkuk 1:12,14: *". . . O Lord, thou hast ordained them for judgment; and, O Mighty God, thou hast established them for correction. . . And makest men as the fishes of the sea, as the creeping things, that have no ruler over them?"* God's watchers have the appearance of that part of the life of creation over which their responsibility lies. Satan appeared in the Garden of Eden in the form of a snake, and one of his names is "the dragon," or "that old serpent." Satan's promotion left a vacancy within the order of watchers which has never been filled, probably as the result of a curse that God put on the creeping and crawling things because of Satan's sin.

5. The fifth and last promotion of Lucifer was doubtless to the rank of an archangel. Only the archangels are named, and Lucifer was Satan's name when he fell. *"How art thou fallen from heaven, O Lucifer . . . "* Lucifer had a throne, and only archangels were given thrones because of their princely positions. *"I will exalt my throne above the stars of God . . . "* (Isaiah 14:13). Satan commanded an army of one-third of the angelic hosts, and only archangels are said to command the armies of God (Revelation 12:3-9).

There is no doubt that Lucifer was the most intelligent and beautiful angel in God's entire universe. He was found perfect in service (Ezekiel 28:15). God recognized Lucifer's capabilities and rewarded him accordingly, yet he became ambitious and would stop at nothing to extend his own kingdom (which God had given him) over the entire universe.

With the rebellion of Lucifer, the spirit world was divided into two opposing forces. According to Ezekiel 28:18, Satan and his angels hold fortified territories in the heavens from which they wage war against the Kingdom of God and Earth. This is the subject of Paul's warning in Ephesians 6:11,12: *"Put on the whole armour of God, that ye may be able to stand against the wiles of the devil. For we wrestle not against flesh and blood, but against principalities, against powers, against the rulers of the darkness of this world, against spiritual wickedness in high places."*

Never have visible manifestations of this unseen war been so evident as in our day. A few years ago the American Medical Association issued a warning against people becoming involved in the occult movement that is sweeping across the world. This supreme medical authority warned that both mental and physical health could be destroyed. There is only one power in Heaven and in Earth that can overcome these evil agents of Satan, and that is the power of the blood of Jesus Christ. I John 5:5,6 says: *"Who is he that overcometh the world, but he that believeth that Jesus is the Son of God? This is he that came by water and blood . . . ."*

Blood of Babylon

The first man to be possessed by Satan was Cain. Cain *"was of that wicked one"* (I John 3:12) and he murdered his brother Abel (Matt. 23:35). The blood of Abel's sacrifice was a prototype of the "Lamb of God" who would take away the sins of the world. Once Abel had placed his faith in the blood, Satan used Cain to take away the blood of his brother in an attempt to eliminate the gospel of the blood atonement. Thereafter, the struggle for man's redemption (through faith in the shed blood of the Redeemer) and the deception of Satan to keep man in a state of eternal condemnation before God revolved around the blood.

Because the blood of Abel's sacrifice had established the type (redemption through the poured-out blood of Jesus Christ on the Cross), man was forbidden to consume the blood of animals: *"But flesh with the life thereof, which is in the blood thereof, shall ye not eat"* (Gen. 9:4). Thus, the "gospel of redemption" was proclaimed in the shedding of blood for the salvation of the soul; and contrariwise, the dirge of Satan related to the consumption of blood unto perdition.

The Israelites, God's chosen witness in the world prior to the Cross were forbidden to eat blood: *"For the life of the flesh is in the blood: and I have given it to you upon the altar to make an atonement for your souls: for it is the blood that maketh an atonement for the soul. Therefore I said unto the children of Israel, No soul of you shall eat blood, neither shall any stranger that sojourneth among you eat blood"* (Lev. 17:11-12). This was passed on to the New Testament church as an ordinance: *"But that we write unto them, that they* (Gentile believers) *abstain from pollutions of idols, and from fornication, and from things strangled, and from blood"* (Acts 15:20). The attack of Satan today comes mainly from these same three sources: 1. Idols (heathen religions — particularly from the East); 2. Fornication (sexual promiscuity which is destroying the home and the witness of Christians); 3. Blood (disputing the blood atonement of Christ).

The drinking of blood and the use of blood in satanic worship to mock the blood atonement of Jesus Christ before the world can be traced all the way back to Sodom and Gomorrah and earlier. The vampirish practice of the defilement of blood, sexual orgies, and worship of Satan have always been joined together. In 1440 A.D., Gilles de Laval, the escort of Joan of Arc, was burned alive for sacrificing young boys to Satan, after he had forced them to submit to homosexual acts. He drained the blood of his innocent victims into large copper vessels, which he later used in the Black Mass. Joan herself was not above suspicion, and she was finally burned at the stake for persisting in dressing like a man, a sin contrary to nature. Madame de Montespan, the mistress of Louis XIV, cut the throats of children and used the blood in satanic masses to enhance her sexual prowess over the king.

Ex-satanist Michael Warnke is quoted in the *Occult Observer* as describing worship of the devil: *"to get blood to drink, we cut inch-long slits in wrists and let them bleed into the chalice. Then we added wine and holy water desecrated with urine. We three priests nibbled the Holy Bread, then passed the chalice around. If we couldn't get fresh blood, you could use menstrual blood. It seems gross now, but somehow it doesn't seem gross if you are doing it as a satanist. You just get psyched out. There is no grossness to it."*

Space and time prohibit a more detailed account of blood sacrifices and sexual defilement in specific cases of satanic worship practiced down through the centuries. However, we do know that from 1950 to the present, there has been a steady increase in reports of both animal and human sacrifices used in devil worship. These steadily growing reports are evidence of the spread of the devil's agents over the face of the Earth. One of the most unusual and alarming of these reports was carried on page 1 of the February 10, 1975 edition of the *Oklahoma City Times:*

"... in Texas stories and reports of mysterious mutilations of cattle, possibly by a blood-drinking Satanist group, are sweeping the country ... There has even been speculation that the puzzling killings were the work of creatures from outer space and flying saucer reports have increased in that area. The mysterious slaughtering, in which such parts as the udder, tongue, and sexual organs are removed and the blood drained, have little or no precedent ... Reports have come from a half-dozen east Texas counties of similar mutilations and investigators say there have been many of the same nature in Iowa, Kansas, and Nebraska. Sheriff Paul Jones of Sulphur Springs in Hopkins County, TX, is one of those who feels the crimes are the acts of an occult Satanist group. 'We found out this much,' Jones said, 'A part of the ceremonial rite is drinking the blood and often decapitating whatever is killed.'"

The article continues to report specific cases of animal mutilations – the tongue, ears and sex organs were removed in each case. But more interesting and puzzling is how the Satanists remove the blood. Whether they suck the blood directly from the animals or use some method unknown at this time to draw the blood is not known. The report in the February 10 edition of the *Oklahoma City Times* continues:

"A Charolais bull was found in Anderson County ... with its sex organs, excretory organs, ears and tongue missing. The bull's hide on one shoulder had been peeled back and all blood had been drained from the carcass in an unexplained manner. Very little or no blood at all is being found about the mutilated animals, indicating that it is being consumed or taken away in containers of some sort ... Texas officials, attempting to deal with the crimes and the wild wave of stories they have brought, were ready to warn every state that officers should watch out."

According to the preceding article, recent animal mutilations follow the same pattern and practice followed by Satanists for thousands of years. In recent years there have been numerous reports of human sacrifices offered by devil worshippers to the god of this world. In fact, human sacrifices are preferred. We wonder how long it will be before Satanists become numerous enough and bold enough to begin sacrificing people and drinking their blood, in great numbers.

The *Minot Daily News* of November 5, 1979 carried an interesting article that is related to the spread of Satanism, blood-related devil worship, and human sacrifices. Much of the article is based on information contained in the November 5, 1979 edition of the Southwest Radio Church publication *The Gospel Truth*. We quote from the newspaper account:

"David Berkowitz, who has refused to cooperate in a new 'Son of Sam' probe by Queens, NY district attorneys, has broken his silence by writing a Ward County deputy that investigators are fighting 'a losing battle' with the forces of witchcraft and Satanism. Berkowitz thus appears to have confirmed that the new investigation's focus on the possibility that the... killings were occult-motivated is correct. Berkowitz sent his eerie message to Ward County Deputy Lt. Terry Gardner from Attica State Prison in New York, where he is serving a 315-year sentence after confessing to killing six people and wounding seven others in the year long 1976-77 shooting spree. Gardner is assigned to investigate the 1978 shooting death of John Carr, the son of Sam Carr, of Yonkers, NY. Sam Carr was Berkowitz's neighbor and so-called master who, Berkowitz asserts, ordered him to kill. John Carr, a former sergeant at Minot Air Force Base, died of a gunshot wound at an air base residence on Feb. 16, 1978 six months after Berkowitz's arrest. John Carr's death was termed an 'apparent suicide' but police now believe he may have been murdered because of his possible involvement in the killings... David Berkowitz, confessed 'Son of Sam' killer, sent this material to Ward County Deputy Sheriff Terry Cardner. The Gospel Truth, a publication of the Southwest Radio Church, based in Oklahoma City, OK, describes 'demonic activity' and warns that 'Satanists are spreading over our nation.' Berkowitz told Gardner, 'All this is just to let you know what your (sic) up against...' "

Berkowitz had previously written a letter to The Southwest Radio Church dated October 20, 1979, in which he stated, *"... at one time I was a member of an occult group. This group contained a mixture of Satanic practices,... it was totally blood oriented... the reason I have chosen to write you is because some unknown person has put my name on your mailing list for literature. I have read many of your materials and I believe now that you are knowledgeable in the field I am talking about. You also seem trustworthy and reliable..."*

David Berkowitz asked us to keep his letter in confidence because his own life and the lives of his family would be in danger if the information was made known. However, when he sent our publication to the authorities investigating Satanic activities, and revealed his own past associations with them, we felt that we were released from any confidentiality in the matter.

It is interesting to note that Mystery Babylon, the satanic religious system of the Tribulation, will be composed of the demon-possessed. This world church of the Tribulation will worship Satan as its god and cause all who do not worship Satan and the Antichrist to be beheaded. In view of Revelation 17:5,6, we might wonder if the blood mentioned is literally the blood of the saints that has been consumed by the members of Satan's church: *"And upon her forehead was a name written MYSTERY, BABYLON THE GREAT, THE MOTHER OF HARLOTS AND ABOMINATIONS OF THE EARTH. And I saw the woman drunken with the blood of the saints, and with the blood of the martyrs of Jesus . . . "*

We read again of this satanic religious system in Revelation 18:24: *"And in her was found the blood of prophets, and of saints, and all that were slain upon the earth."*

Martin Luther said that according to the Scriptures, there would be a great upsurge in satanic activity upon the Earth as the return of the Lord Jesus Christ approached. G. Campbell Morgan contended that he could already see the approaching demonic invasion in his day. The reason we expect such a satanic onslaught, carrying before it everything that is sacred, stable, and holy, is because God's Word has warned us to be ready for it. Jesus said of the last days in Matthew 24:24: *"For there shall arise false Christs, and false prophets, and shall shew great signs and wonders . . . "* No false Christ or false prophet can do miracles except by the power of Satan.

Paul wrote in I Timothy 4:1: *"Now the Spirit speaketh expressly, that in the latter times some shall depart from the faith, giving heed to seducing spirits, and doctrines of devils."* Paul wrote again in II Thess. 2:6-8: *"And now ye know what withholdeth that he might be revealed in his time. For the mystery of iniquity doth already work: only he who now letteth will let, until he be taken out of the way. And then shall that Wicked be revealed, whom the Lord shall consume with the spirit of his mouth, and shall destroy with the brightness of his coming."* In this Scripture, Paul wrote by inspiration of God before the Antichrist is revealed, there must come a rise in iniquity (lawlessness). This prophecy is amplified in the third chapter of II Timothy which begins: *"This know also, that in the last days, perilous times shall come."* The apostle continued to inform us of the rise of sexual perversion in the last days and an overturning of institutions and relationships established by God.

Concerning the alarming rise in Satanism and witchcraft in the United States, we quote from the January 1983 edition of *Moody Monthly:*

"Sixteen years ago, Anton LaVey, author of the satanic bible, started the First Church of Satan in San Francisco.

"In 1970, the University of California at Berkely awarded a bachelor of arts degree with a major in magic to Isaac Bonewits. This magick (spelled with a 'k' according to witchcraft sources) is not the illusional sleight-of-hand kind, but supernatural. Bonewits is a druid, or witch.

"Today, more than 450 identifiable groups are involved in sorcery (witchcraft, satanism, voodoo) in America. 'Sorcery in the narrow sense is magic

used with evil intent to cause damage or death or to win the unlawful or forbidden.' the New Schaff-Herzog Encyclopedia of Religious Knowledge (vol. 15, p. 1048) says.

"New York, Illinois, Ohio and Wisconsin join California as the five states where sorcerers are most active today. But Satanism is found all across the country – in Los Angeles, San Francisco, Chicago, Toledo, Indianapolis, Louisville, New York, St. Petersburg, Sedona in Arizona, and Racine and Kenosha in Wisconsin. Voodoo is practiced in Miami (Newsweek magazine, June 22, 1981, documents the problem), New Orleans, Harlem and Chicago.

"The sorcerer, a medium, uses his mind as a bridge to communicate with 'intangible forces' or 'spirits.' These spirits are crafty and evil from the Christian perspective. God says that 'in latter times some will fall away from the faith, paying attention to deceitful spirits and doctrines of demons' (I Tim. 4:1). The sorcerer receives messages from the spirit or demon world.

"The word witch comes from the Anglo-Saxon term wicca, which means 'one who knows' or 'wise one.' This wise one calls upon the 'forces of nature' for scripturally forbidden purposes.

"The forces of nature (called 'gods or goddesses' by witches) are mentioned in Ephesians 6:12 – 'For our struggle is not against flesh and blood, but against the rulers, against the powers, against the world forces of this darkness, against the spiritual forces of wickedness in the heavenly places.' These are various ranks of fallen angels now opposing God ... Witchcraft groups cling closely to the skirt of the women's liberation movement. The Los Angeles Times (April 10, 1978) covered a three-day extension course listed as 'The Great Goddess Re-emerging' at the University of California at Santa Cruz.

" 'Nearly 400 women picked different notes and held them, catching their breaths at different times so the sound droned unabated for five minutes,' the report said.

" 'The eerie monotones from this congregation of sorts reverberated against the angular outside walls of the Theater of Performing Arts and filtered through clumps of tall pines. The hymnic call was to the goddess.

" 'Later in the day, encouraged by the beat of bongo drums, spontaneous groups of circling women danced ... in scenes suggestive of frolicking wood nymphs.

" 'Surprised sponsors had to turn away potential registrants after the maximum 450 spaces were filled. Although the lectures were mostly academic, the gathering had the spirit of a feminist rally and the body contact of an encounter weekend. Cheers and whoops went up for the goddesses of yore – Isis, Astara, Demeter, Artemis, etc.

" 'Likewise, there was applause for articulate or artistic use of divine female imagery to support contemporary women's self-esteem. More than a successful university extension course, however, the event was indicative of a burgeoning spiritual dimension to the women's liberation movement in America.'

"In the summer of 1981, a citywide 'women's spirituality conference' was *held in Milwaukee. Conducted in a church, the seminar incorporated witchcraft philosophy. One lecturer, Mary Ann Ihm, spoke about a supernatural vision she had of the goddess Eva. Ihm claims in her resume that she chairs the Feminist Spirituality Task Force of NOW's Women and Religion Committee."*

Satan is using every means possible, every cause, to promote his own Kingdom of Darkness on this earth. Satan knows that his time is short, and his demonic hordes are working overtime. But Christians can take comfort in the assurance given in I John 4:4: *". . . greater is he that is in you, than he that is in the world."*

As God's children, we are commanded to stick close to Jesus in these last days: *". . . If we walk in the light, as he is in the light, we have fellowship one with another, and the blood of Jesus Christ his Son cleanseth us from all sin"* (I John 1:7).

Satan's Music

We read of the time just before Christ returns in Revelation 12:12: *"Therefore rejoice, ye heavens, and ye that dwell in them. Woe to the inhabiters of the earth and of the sea! for the devil is come down unto you, having great wrath, because he knoweth that he hath but a short time."*

We can be sure that Satan knows the lateness of the hour and that the time is near when he shall be deprived of his kingdom here on Earth and cast into the bottomless pit (Rev. 20:1-3). The wicked one, like an unchained dragon fighting as he is herded into a cage, lashes out with all the evil forces at his command. We quote John P. Newport from his book, *Demons, Demons, Demons* (Broadman Press):

"Is this a demonic age? It is in the sense there appears to be a struggle — both cosmic and historical — moving toward a crescendo — between the forces of God and the forces of the satanic powers. This development can be seen in a dramatic way in the contemporary youth culture. There is a struggle between those young people using folk-rock music who look to Jesus for inspiration and those who look to Satan for meaning . . . The lyrics of such groups as the Rolling Stones talk about sympathy for the devil. The Black Sabbath, a rock celebration of sorcery and witchcraft, has had international appeal."

Our nation is undergoing an onslaught of sounds from the bottomless pit; the sicker and more satanic it is, the greater the reception. We have even had satanic rock accompanied by blood-letting and snakes. The minds of this generation are being prepared to accept the "man of sin" spoken of in II Thess. 2:3,4: *"Let no man deceive you by any means: for that day shall not come, except there come a falling away first, and that man of sin be revealed, the son of perdition; Who opposeth and exalteth himself above all that is called God, or that is worshipped; so that he as God sitteth in the temple of God, shewing himself that he is God."*

Convincing evidence of the spread of Satanism over the world today in preparation for the reign of Antichrist is beyond controversy. Church leaders like Martin Luther have taught for centuries that according to the Scriptures, a massive invasion of evil spirits would occur in the last days. In 1950, Wilbur M. Smith called to the attention of Christians, the fact that the predicted demonic invasion was at hand. In 1952, Merrill Unger published his work entitled *Biblical Demonology* to forewarn and forearm Christians to meet the coming satanic assault. It came in with a flood in the 60's, and Anton LaVey, titular head of the Church of Satan, was quoted as saying: *"The Satanic Age started in 1966. That's when God was proclaimed dead, the Sexual Freedom League came into prominence, and the hippies developed as a free sex culture."*

An article by Dr. Max Rafferty, well-known educator, carried by local daily newspapers several years ago, stated in part: *"Those rock 'festivals' are really death traps ... Isn't it about time we normal Americans outlawed these damnable 'rock festivals'? ... These deafening, dope-ridden, degenerate mob scenes have no more place in our America than would a publicly promoted gang rape or a legally sanctioned performance of the Black Mass ... A few bewildered sheriff's deputies are assigned to police tens of thousands of hopped-up sex maniacs, and wind up stunned by the decibel level, daunted by dire threats against their lives and discouraged by the sheer magnitude of the problem which confronts them. Result: the laws end up uninforced ... This is an absolutely intolerable and completely dastardly situation. The numbers of the criminals involved in the commission of a crime should have no bearing whatever upon the enforcement of the law."* (Macomb Daily, 8/24/70).

This noted educator was not necessarily prophetic, only observant. How many young people, since this warning, have had their minds destroyed by drugs, their faith and purpose in life obliterated, or even committed suicide, as a result of contemporary rock and disco music may never be known. Many experts believe the figures would run into the millions, and world-wide, the statistics could be in the hundreds of millions. Frank Garlock, in his book *The Big Beat*, states on page 11:

The disciples of chaos and disorder could not have found a more perfect vehicle to promote and instill their ideas and philosophies in a generation of young people. The two countries where rock 'n' roll is most popular, the United States and England, have not only the highest juvenile delinquency rates in the world but also have the greatest increase in juvenile crime rate, in illegitimate birth rate, and in over-all crime rate, and the worst suicide rate in the world. According to a United Press report (Greenville News 2/28/68). 'As a cause of teen-age deaths in the United States, suicide now outranks polio, pneumonia, tuberculosis, diabetes, rheumatic fever, kidney disease, appendicitis and leukemia. Among college students, suicide is second only to motor vehicle accidents as the most frequent cause of death.' ... After his daughter's death in 1969, Art Linkletter blamed 'secret messages' in rock music lyrics for encouraging young people to take part in the growing problem of drug abuse."

Although there are exceptions, most lyrics for rock music peddle revolution, hatred for parents and all authority, sex, drugs, depression and suicide. While parents may not be able to understand the words to the music because of the heavy beat or terminologies which disguise their true meaning, the message is there and teen-agers understand it. Tom Allen, in an article that appeared in *Herald Of His Coming* (January 1978) wrote:

"There are five major themes in the world's rock 'n' roll music – sex, drugs, rebellion, false religion (usually Eastern religion) and devils. There has been a subliminal attack on the mind of many of us through rock music. It has been a secretative move of the devil. I myself was caught in this ... It is true that in a lot of rock music you cannot discern the words consciously – but that is the trick! That is where we have been fooled! We are learning them subconsciously.

Today I can quote several songs because, although at the time I listened, the lyrics were mysterious and foggy, yet after the subconscious had a long enough time to discern and sort them out, the conscious mind knew what I was listening to. I went to the psychologist on campus and asked him about this subconscious business. I asked if the words were really getting hold of my mind, if I was really listening to words that I couldn't hear outwardly and yet they were coming into my mind inwardly. The psychologist said, 'Undoubtedly, yes!' "

Concerning the origin of rock music, we refer again to the book *The Big Beat*, page 22: *"All one needs to do is to make a trip to the places where rock 'n' roll has its roots (Africa, South America, and India) and observe the ceremonies which often go along with this kind of music – voodoo rituals, sex orgies, human sacrifice, and devil worship – to know the direction in which we as a nation are headed."*

The claims by many rock musicians parallels those described by Bob Larson in the book *The Day Music Died: "It happens to us quite often – it feels as though I'm not playing my instrument, so something else is playing it and that same thing is playing all three of our instruments. That's what I mean when I say it's frightening sometimes. Maybe we'll all play the same phrase from out of nowhere. It happens very often with us."*

The author of *Pot, Rock and Revolution* provides the following description of the effect of the rock beat on the mind: *"It has been found that the dance strobe lights, when flashed at the rate of 6 to 8 cycles per second, result in loss of depth perception. At 25 cycles per second, the flashing interferes with the alpha waves which control the ability of the brain to concentrate. Probably the simplest description of what happens to the youngsters is described by Dr. Joost A. M. Meerlo, M.D., in his book 'Rape of the Mind.' Dr. Meerlo says, 'Violent raucous noise produces violent emotional reactions and destroys control.'*

"Former rock player Bob Larson, in conjunction with a physician, offers some light on the relationship between 'hard rock' and promiscuous sex. He contends that the low frequency vibrations of the bass guitar, coupled with the driving beat of the drum, have a decided effect upon the cerebrospinal fluid. The fluid in turn affects the pituitary gland which directs the secretion of hormones, resulting in an abnormal balance of sex and adrenalin hormones. Instead of their normal regulatory function, these hormones produce radical changes in the blood sugar, it ceases to function properly, causing moral inhibitions to either drop to a dangerous low or be wiped out altogether."

Having discussed the ethical aspects of hard rock music in the first part of this study, we now turn to a new type that has emerged in the last few years – disco. One of the reasons for the newer type of rock was to accommodate a broadening of sexual freedom to include the gays. This does not mean that all who go to disco parlors are homosexuals, but many of them are. The Jaunary,1978 edition of *Discoworld*, in an article titled "Disco's Gay Roots," made the following observation:

"Some readers will recognize that many of the discotheques listed are gay

discos or gay clubs. 'Billboard' magazine (a prominent entertainment trade journal) has estimated that at least 50 percent of the discotheques in the country are gay, which is not surprising since the disco movement got its primary impetus from the gay community. Invariably, as news about a new gay club with great sound and decor gets around, straight people who want to dance start knocking at the door."

An article that appeared recently in the press proves without reservation how Satan is using rock music as a medium to demonize the younger generation. We quote from an AP news release that appeared in the April 28, 1982 edition of the Press-Telegram, Long Beach, California:

BILL BEDEVILED BY SKEPTICS

"SACRAMENTO (AP) – The Assembly committee members leaned forward Tuesday as a Colorado researcher played a tape of a Led Zeppelin rock song backward.

"The song, 'Stairway To Heaven,' turned into cacophony on the backward tape, interspersed with mumbled words, such as 'Here's to my sweet Satan' and 'I live for Satan.'

"William Yarroll told the committee the subconscious mind can decipher the backward message hidden in the song even when the record is played forward. The message, placed there by rock musicians in league with satanists, is accepted by the brain as fact, he contended.

"The Consumer Protection and Toxic Materials Committee was interested but skeptical and recommended more study for a bill that would require warning labels on records with subliminal messages recorded backward.

"Committee chairwoman Sally Tanner, D-El Monte, said the entire subject of subliminal messages was 'exciting and interesting' and should be considered at a hearing in the fall.

"She said the recording industry, musicians and other scientists who have studied the matter should be invited to testify.

"The author of the bill, Assemblyman Phil Wyman, R-Tehachapi, said backward messages on records, called backward masking, 'can manipulate our behavior without our knowledge or consent and turn us into disciples of the anti-Christ.'

"He said scientists have known for some time about subliminal advertising, whereby messages that cannot be consciously perceived but are noticed only by the subconscious are flashed on movie or television screens.

"He said he introduced the bill when a constituent, Monika Wilfley of Lancaster, came to him complaining about backward messages on rock records.

"Ms. Wilfley, who described herself as 'a 20-year-old mother,' said she saw a Christian television program that described Yarroll's research.

"She said she then went home and played some of her rock records backward and heard the satanic messages Yarroll described.

" 'We threw away a lot of records and tapes and such. It was really *frustrating. Some of them were new,' she said.*

"Yarroll, who has a research firm called Applied Potentials Institute in Aurora, CO, said the subconscious part of the brain can understand a backward message and 'store it as the truth.'

"He said the rock artists add the backward tracks to their records because 'the Church of Satan and their followers have a pact that if you perform certain things in your particular line of work, in return Satan will give you certain favors back.'

"Yarroll said that in research at the University of Colorado Health Sciences Center he found some of the backward phrases from rock records repeated in young people's suicide notes.

"The tapes Yarroll played included the words 'Turn me on dead man' from the song 'Revolution No. 9' by the Beatles, the words 'The music is reversible, but time isn't' from 'Face The Music' by Electric Light Orchestra and 'Satan, Satan, Satan, he is god' from 'Raunch 'n' Roll' by Black Oak Arkansas."

Satan has a cheap counterfeit for every beautiful creation or expression of God. The Psalmists writes: *"Make a joyful noise unto God, all ye lands"* (Psalm 66:1). It is only natural that Satan would pollute the airwaves with his counterfeit music. Often, without thinking, Christians invite such Satanic deception into their own churches, homes, or minds. Once again we need to keep before us Paul's instructions in Ephesians 6:11: *"Put on the whole armour of God, that ye may be able to stand against the wiles of the devil."*

Servants of Satan

We are admonished by the Scriptures to resist all the wiles of the devil, because Satan uses many devices to add souls to his kingdom. God also tells us in His Word about Satan and his angels, and the Bible mentions demon possession repeatedly. "Demons" in the English language is sometimes rendered "devils," meaning agents of the devil.

The scope of eschatology reflects an increase in demonic and fallen angelic activity in the latter years. In the past decade a large number of books on increasing satanic manifestations by noted Christian theologians and authors have poured from the presses. These books warn that the devil today is indeed going about like a roaring lion, seeking those whom he may devour (I Peter 5:8). We quote from just a few of these:

Angels and Demons by Needham (Moody Press): *"Satan's master stroke of policy is to divert our minds from inquiry concerning his true character and the methods by which he governs his kingdom. His resources are so varied and his modes of operation so elastic that it is extremely difficult to determine the bounds of his authority. Sometimes he employs the vehicle of darkness to blind the minds of those who do not believe, lest the light of the Gospel of the glory of Christ should dawn upon them (II Cor. 4:4). And sometimes, unto those who do believe the Gospel, he transforms himself into an angel of light, that thus, by bewildering, he may delude them into his snares (II Cor. 11:14)."*

The Occult Explosion by Wilson (Master Books): *"Is it primitive superstition, just so much nonsense – or are there really evil spirits in the world around us? In this book I say there are such spirits, and I present some of the evidence. I show some of the subtle ways in which they manifest themselves. Sometimes they even materialize... they can and do utilize psychological principles, while at other times their influence is essentially in the spiritual realm. The fact is that ALL their activities are intrusions into the spiritual, for that is the ultimate reality. The devil and his demons know that if one method of attack fails, they will use another. They have patience, they have skill, and they have hatred – hatred of God and hatred of man because he is God's crown of creation. Today they have come out into the open. They have initiated an assault in ways that a generation ago would have seemed unthinkable."*

The Program of Satan by Schwarze (Good News Publishers): *"The Devil has changed his public image. He's no longer a comical character with pointed ears, a pitch-fork and hooves. Satan has exposed himself. Today he's the leading character in bestselling novels and successful films. People worship him in elaborate black masses. Do-it-yourself books on Satanism are invading suburbia. Courses on the Occult and Astrology are offered in some school districts."*

Satan Is Alive and Well on Planet Earth by Lindsey (Bantam Books): *"Witchcraft and Satan worship spread throughout campuses and cities. In America, a so-called civilized country, people are involved in weird rites and rituals. We are all part of an unseen conflict in the world and within ourselves... Consider what is said about this clever character, Satan. Anyone who has dominated history as he has cannot be ignored, especially in these days. To do so may be at the peril of your very life."*

So that we may know our enemy, let us identify the powers and rulers of darkness whom Satan is using to corrupt the masses even as he did in the days of Noah.

ASTROLOGERS

Satan operates on the theory that every man has his price, and he offers something for everybody. Perhaps the most inoffensive and seemingly harmless of the agents of Satan are the astrologers. Movie stars, millionaires, congressmen, kings, and men of renown in all areas of politics, economics, the arts, and even religion, depend upon their horoscopes for guidance in daily affairs. Yet, the Bible does not have one good word to say about an astrologer or the false science of astrology. Isaiah 47:13,14 says: *". . . Let now the astrologers, the stargazers, the monthly prognosticators, stand up, and save thee from these things that shall come upon thee. Behold, they shall be as stubble; the fire shall burn them; they shall not deliver themselves from the power of the flame . . . "*

It is also evident from the first, second, fourth, and fifth chapters of Daniel that astrologers are the agents of Satan, and a rise in astrology always precedes demon possession and the moral disintegration of a nation. Astrology can be traced back to Babel, and even further back to the antediluvians. Paul wrote in Romans 1:23 that God condemns all those who change the glory of God's creation into "an image made like to corruptible man, and to birds, and fourfooted beasts, and creeping things" (symbols in the zodiac). The apostle says that God gives such deceived people up to vile affections, crime, and sexual perversions. Astrology precedes moral disintegration and Satanic destruction. It is no coincidence, in light of national moral decay, that astrology is booming. In 1953, only about 100 newspapers carried horoscope columns. Twenty years later, approximately 2,000 newspapers carried daily horoscopes, and there were almost 200,000 professional astrologers. In other nations the percentage of the population that reads their daily horoscope and patronizes astrologers is as follows: Britain, 66%; France, 53%; Germany, 63% *(Cults and the Occult* by Gruss).

SORCERY

The root word for "sorcery" in the Greek text means "pharmacy" or "drugs" in English. Sorcerers have always used drugs (called magic potions) to cause vision, or as we would say today, hallucinations. Sorcerers, and all those who engage in traffic with sorcerers, are condemned in God's Word. Jeremiah 27:9, Isaiah 47:9, Daniel 2:2, and many other Old Testament Scriptures identify sorcerers as agents of Satan. Elymas the sorcerer of Acts 13 is called a "child of the devil" (v. 10). But it is remarkable that the sorcerers predicted for the last days in Revelation are most strictly defined in the Greek as merchants of drugs *(Young's Analytical Concordance)*. Revelation 9:13-21 depicts the widespread use of drugs in the last days, causing murder, sexual depravity, robbery, demon possession, and devil worship. We read in Revelation 18:23 that all nations will have a serious drug problem just before Christ returns. The reduced penalty for marijuana possession in our own country is another example of Satan working behind the scenes.

An example of drug addiction causing demon possession was carried in *Decision*, in an article entitled "Exit The Monkey Demon." The young man whose personal testimony of demon possession was recorded in the article said: *"I am convinced that anyone who has taken LSD (the same applies to other drugs) for any amount of time is possessed by some principle of evil, and the only one who can cast out demons is Jesus Christ."* Sorcerers, or drug merchants, are sixth on the list of those for whom is reserved the hottest fires of Hell (Rev. 21:8). Drugs are the devil's medicine for the last days, and certainly one of the wiles of the evil one to corrupt the world.

WITCHES

According to the book *Demons, Demons, Demons* by John Newport (Broadman Press), in 1972 there were at least 5,000 witches in New York, 10,000 in Los Angeles, and in the entire United States there were one half as many witches as clergymen. In view of the declining membership in the churches of many of the larger denominations and the rise of witchcraft, it may be just a matter of time until witches outnumber clergymen. In England, France, Germany, and other nations in Europe, witchcraft is reported to be even more widespread than in the United States.

God identifies witches in the Bible as agents of Satan, and the Israelites were commanded to put a witch to death (Exodus 22:18). The acceptance of witches as the more respectable members of the new occult society testifies to the fact that Satan is tightening his grip upon the world in preparation for the coming struggle. He will then make his final effort to exalt his kingdom of darkness above the Kingdom of God.

PROGNOSTICATORS

Predictions by Jeanne Dixon, Sibyl Leek, Maurice Woodruff, Edgar Cayce, and a host of other prognosticators, clairvoyants, and seers have filled the newspapers during the past decade. Jeanne Dixon is consultant to some of the most prominent figures in the arts and politics, and she is one of the best-known people in the world today. Her widespread popularity and common identifiability testifies to her acceptance as a credible prophet. She uses astrology, the crystal ball, ESP, and vision — the whole occult ball-of-wax that is condemned over and over in the Bible. Yet she wrote in her book *The Call To Glory:* "*It is my belief God has given me a gift of prophecy for His own reasons . . . God talks to me. I know then, beyond all doubt, that the channel is coming directly to me from the Divine, the Lord our God.*" Of all the modern prognosticators, Miss Dixon claims the highest percentage of accurancy, approximately 80 percent. But what of the approximate 20 percent which she misses? Are these of God also? If so, then God would be a liar. A true biblical prophet to whom God gave insight into the future by the Holy Spirit was never wrong, but was 100 percent accurate — this is the test of a true prophet of God (Deut. 18:20-22).

Prognosticators are identified in Isaiah 47:13 with those who are of Satan and who lead the unwary away from God's Word for wisdom concerning those things which are coming upon the Earth. Yet it is probable that most people read the forecasts of modern prognosticators more than they consult the "*. . . more sure word of prophecy . . . a light that shineth in a dark place . . .*" (II Peter 1:19). In her more recent visions, Jeanne Dixon predicts a glorious world in the near future through reincarnation, but she overlooks the coming judgments of the Great Tribulation.

SPIRITISTS

Spiritists, also called mediums, are those who claim contact with the world of the departed dead through the medium of familiar spirits. Spiritists have become popular in these last days along with all the other deceivers of Satan. In 1967 a well-known medium, Arthur Ford, was on a television show with the late Bishop James Pike, and millions across the nation were involved in this "trip to the spirit domain." Through the televised experience of these two men, countless adherents to spiritism were gained. The religious posture of Bishop Pike deceived many, even some who professed Christ as Lord and Saviour. Spiritism continues to gain acceptance by an increasing number of people.

God identifies those who seek to contact the dead through familiar spirits as in league with the devil. Isaiah 8:19,22 says: "*And when they shall say unto you, Seek unto them that have familiar spirits, and unto wizards that peep, and that mutter: should not a people seek unto their God? for the living to the dead? . . . And they shall look unto the earth; and behold trouble and darkness, dimness of anguish; and they shall be driven to darkness.*"

DEMONS

Besides the fallen angels of Satan's kingdom there are demons. Satan is nowhere in the Bible ascribed to have the power to create life in any form; therefore, it may seem a mystery as to where demons originated. Due to the fact that demons have no bodies, and desire the bodies of the living (humans or animals), some believe that they are the spirits of the half-angels and half-humans that resulted from the union between the fallen angels of Genesis 6:2 and woman on Earth. Their bodies were destroyed in the Flood, but their spirits continued to live. Regardless of their origin, demons are identified in the Bible as real, and as servants of Satan; until the day of their judgment by Jesus Christ (Matt. 8:29). Satan is called Beelzebub, the prince of demons (Matt. 12:24).

People become demon-possess when they place themselves on Satan's ground, and this is evidently why many on drugs fall prey to these agents of the bottomless pit. The existence of demons was classified by the scientific community as superstition, but demon possession has become so evident today that few bother to deny their existence. The motion picture *The Exorcist*, and other like movies, dramatized before millions the reality and torture of demon possession. Demon possession is referred to in I Timothy 4:1: *"Now the Spirit speaketh expressly, that in the latter times some shall depart from the faith, giving heed to seducing spirits, and doctrines of devils."*

One college professor boldy dresses up like the Devil to propose what we consider Satanic programs to his students. Quoting from the November 7, 1982 edition of *Savannah News-Press:*

"When professor Newtol Press dons his plastic horns, he may suggest that all people in the world should look alike or that some poor people should be sterilized. He plays devil's advocate in an attempt to goad his students into thought, and officials at the University of Milwaukee say his bioethecs course is popular. 'I'll suggest sterilizing welfare mothers, killing the elderly to save money,' Press said. 'Many of the students were a little perplexed, a little disoriented to find out they would actually have to solve problems like this. But they say they enjoy thinking and this is one of the few courses that enables them to do that.' Press, 51, decided to play the role of the devil's advocate about five years ago when he and other teachers were looking for a way to get their students to do more than just repeat information." The Bible predicts an influx of demons upon the world from the bottomless pit in the last days to possess those who have turned from God and accepted Satan as their master (Rev. 9:1-12). Demonic activity today bears evidence that we are living in the last days.

APOSTATES

Perhaps the most effective agents of the devil are the apostates who stand in the pulpits of the churches. An apostle is one chosen by God to declare that God's Son, Jesus Christ, has come in the flesh. An apostate is one chosen of Satan to deny that Jesus Christ has come in the flesh: *"For such are false apostles, deceitful workers, transforming themselves into the apostles of Christ. And no marvel; for Satan himself is transformed into an angel of light"* (II Cor. 11:13,14). Every preacher today who denies that Jesus Christ is the only begotten Son of God, and denies His atoning death on the Cross, is an agent of Satan working to prepare the way for Antichrist: *"And every spirit that confesseth not that Jesus Christ is come in the flesh is not of God: and this is that spirit of antichrist, whereof ye have heard that it should come; and even now already is it in the world"* (I John 4:3).

Down through the Church Age few ministers, either in the Roman Catholic Church or non-Catholic churches, have had the courage to make such a blasphemous charge against God's Son. Yet today, the majority in Protestant churches do it boastfully and unashamedly every Sunday morning. According to recent clerical polls *(Christianity Today)*, over 50% of the seminary graduates believe that Jesus Christ was only a man, and nothing more. The increasing number of blatant apostates occupying positions as pastors and church officials testifies that Satan is swiftly preparing the world for Antichrist.

TRYING THE SPIRITS

Christians are admonished in I John 4:1,: *"Beloved, believe not every spirit, but try the spirits whether they are of God . . . "* By using the outline in this article, it is possible for you to try the spirits. By Bible definition, astrologers, witches, drug pushers, prognosticators, spiritists, demons, apostates, and a host of others in the growing occult movement of our day, are being used by Satan in an attempt to prevent the glorious return of our Lord Jesus Christ.

Satanists are spreading over our nation offering sacrifices and drinking blood in their damnable Black Masses. Evidence is growing that the Earth is under a severe satanic attack, both from within and from without. The night of the Tribulation must be near at hand. Christians, who are of the day, should be diligent, observing the signs of the times and holding up the Lord Jesus Christ as the only name given among men whereby they must be saved.

"Angel of Light"

The apostle Paul spoke of Satan, the prince of darkness, as transforming himself to appear as an angel of light: *"For such are false apostles, deceitful workers, transforming themselves into the apostles of Christ. And no marvel; for Satan himself is transformed into an angel of light. Therefore it is no great thing if his ministers also be transformed as the ministers of righteousness; whose end shall be according to their works"* (II Cor. 11:13-15).

There have always been false light-bearers to lead men away from the truth, but only a few times in history have these agents of Satan surfaced under an identifiable name. One of these rare occasions was late in the 18th century when an organization dedicated to the eradication of the Gospel of Jesus Christ from the Earth came into being. It was called the Illuminati, which by interpretation is "the illumined ones," or the "followers of the illumined one," the angel of light.

THE ILLUMINATI – ITS LITERAL EXISTENCE

Two of the most reliable sources for documentation acknowledged by most Americans are *Webster's Dictionary* and *The Encyclopaedia Britannica*. *Webster's New Twentieth Century Dictionary, Unabridged*, gives the following definitions:

Illuminate: one pretending to have extraordinary knowledge or skill; one of the illuminati.

Illuminati: . . . the members of an anticlerical, deistic, republican society founded in 1776 by Adam Weishaupt, professor of law at Ingolstadt in Bavaria.

The *Encyclopaedia Britannica* comments on the Illuminati: *"A short-lived movement . . . founded on May Day (May 1) 1776 by Adam Weishaupt . . . a former Jesuit. The members of this secret society called themselves 'Perfectibilists.' Their founder's aim was to replace Christianity by a religion of reason, as later did the revolutionaries of France . . . The order was organized along Jesuit lines and kept internal discipline and a system of surveillance based on that model . . . From 1778 onward, they began to make contact with various Masonic lodges, where, under the impulse of A. Knigge, one of their chief converts, they often managed to gain a commanding position. The total membership never exceeded 2,000."*

The emergence of the Illuminati under the leadership of Weishaupt was short-lived, but evidence clearly indicates that the organization existed centuries before Weishaupt was born, and continues today. The conversion of Weishaupt to Illuminism is documented on pages 100 and 101 of the book *Conspiracy*

Against God and Man, by Rev. Clarence Kelly: *"Considering Weishaupt's knowledge of ancient secret societies, together with the fact that certain aspects of his Order more than superficially resemble the structure of those societies, it seems reasonable to say that he was probably influenced by this knowledge . . . Nesta Webster relates the reflections of the Abbe' Barruel and another writer by the name of Lecouteulx de Canteleu. 'In 1771, they relate a certain Jutland merchant named Kolmer, who had spent many years in Egypt, returned to Europe in search of converts to a secret doctrine founded on Manchaeism that he had learned in the East. On his way to France he stopped at Malta, where he met Cagliostro and nearly brought about an insurrection amongst the people. Kolmer was therefore driven out of the island by the Knights of Malta and betook himself to Avignon and Lyons. Here he made a few disciples amongst the Illumines and in the same year went on to Germany where he encountered Weishaupt and initiated him into all the mysteries of his secret doctrine. According to Barruel, Weishaupt then spent five years thinking out his system, which he founded under the name of Illuminati on May 1, 1776."*

According to the book *Conspiracy Against God and Man*, the doctrine of Weishaupt can be traced back to 872 A.D., to a sect called the Ismailis. But this doctrine, which advocated the overthrow of the existing social order and all forms of religions, and replacing them with a universal dictatorship, goes back even further in time. Quoting from page 202 of the book *Secret Societies and Subversive Movements*, by Nesta H. Webster: *"Illuminism . . . marks an entirely new departure in the history of European secret societies. Weishaupt himself indicates this as one of the great secrets of the Order. 'Above all,' he writes to 'Cato' (alias Zwack), 'guard the origin and the novelty of ⊙ in the most careful way.' 'The greatest mystery,' he says again, 'must be that the thing is new; the fewer who know this the better . . . Not one of the Eichstadters know this but would live or die for it that thing is as old as Methuselah.' "*

Weishaupt identified a mark with the name, beginning, beliefs, and goals of the Illuminati. It was the emblem of the "All-Seeing Eye," a circle with a dot in the middle. Weishaupt himself said that although men would think it was new, it was as old as Methuselah himself. This scheme again illustrates the truth that Satan has never altered his plan. He has not found it necessary to change it, because since Eden it has worked again and again.

THE EMBLEM – ITS HISTORY

The emblem of the Illuminati, as indicated by Weishaupt, antedates the Flood. As we shall discuss in more detail later, the order of the supreme council of the Illuminati works through other organizations and religions to obtain its goals. One of the feeder religions of the order is Rosicrucianism. Rosicrucianism itself claims identification with the Illuminati. According to the book *Cults and the Occult*, by Baker Publishing, H. Spencer Lewis, First Imperator of the religion, wrote in his dissertation titled "Mastery of Life": *"The order had its* birth as one of the mystery schools of secret wisdom in ancient Egypt during the 18th Dynasty, or the reign of Pharaoh Amenhotep IV, about 1350 B.C."

Rosicrucianism is also called the Ancient Mystical Order Rosae Crucis, or the rose on the Cross. This is an obvious attempt to adorn and make the Cross an object of beauty, and thus nullify its meaning to humanity. The Cross of Christ was not beautiful, because it was upon the Cross that the Son of God suffered and died for sin. Nine main emblems were worn by Rosicrucians. The fifth seal is the compass, the very same sign that appears on the Masonic emblem. These identifying symbols appear on page 49 of the *Rosicrucian Official Handbook*. The fourth emblem, called the Seal of the Founder, is composed of three items: (1) On the bottom is a beetle, signifying all living things, including man. (2) Over the beetle is a crown, signifying a single monarch over all the world. (3) Over the crown is a third item — the sign of the "all-seeing eye," exactly the same sign that is identified with the Illuminati. Like the Masons, the Rosicrucians also have "orders," and we read from page 74 of the *Rosicrucian Official Handbook*: *"Members who attain and complete the psychic instruction of the Ninth Degree or those above it may enter the ILLUMINATI, which is a higher organization of the Order wherein the worthy Members continue to carry on specialized work and studies under the direction of the Imperator of their Jurisdiction and the personal Cosmic Masters. Members cannot ask for admission to the Illuminati but must wait until they have been found ready and are invited to share in the additional work."*

Rosicrucianism traces its beginning to ancient Egyptian mysticism. The teacher of Weishaupt who converted him to Illuminism was from Egypt. Rosicrucians, the Masons, and the Illuminati are linked together by organizational structure, emblems, and practices. This cannot be denied by anyone who can add 2 and 2 and get 4 as the answer. Weishaupt used the Masons extensively, which is indicated by *The Encyclopaedia Britannica.* Most of the founders of the United States were either members of the Rosicrucian Mystical Order or Masons. On page 92 of *Cults and the Occult* by Baker Book House, it is reported that Benjamin Franklin was a Rosicrucian. Thomas Jefferson and John Adams were Masons, although Adams and Jefferson later disagreed over the use of the Masonic Lodge by the Illuminati. John Adams, who is reported to be the founder of the Masonic Lodges of New England, accused Jefferson of using the lodges for subversive Illuminati purposes. According to the Cinema Educational Guild of California, the three letters of Adams which deal with this problem are in Wittingburg Square Library in Philadelphia.

This is not to indict any of the American Founding Fathers for being un-Christian or unpatriotic. Considering the forces they had to deal with it is amazing that they laid such a solid foundation for our great nation. God must have guided them through the satanic traps that beset them. We should not construe all Masons to be members of international conspiracy.

Jefferson was idealistic, and many of Weishaupt's ideas corresponded with his own, just as many of the liberal clergy today are deceived by Communism, another offshoot of so-called Illuminism. There are many others who have found themselves to be dupes of the satanic conspiracy. Quoting from page 66 of *The Cosmic Conspiracy,* by Stan Deyo: *"Weishaupt wanted a deistic republic of global dimensions. To those who have read the book entitled 'Protocols of the Learned Elders of Zion' it must be obvious – since the book discussed not only Weishaupt's six points of subversive revolution (and 18 more) – that neither Jewish Elders nor Masons were entirely responsible for writing it. Neither group would have been stupid enough to so obviously indict themselves in such a document – secret or otherwise. The protocols are real; they do exist; and they have been exercised with alarming precision by some groups for more than 100 years. They were truly written by the Illuminati . . . that same Illuminati whose Hermetic code insists on secrecy . . . and a 'low profile.' The Jews and Masons have been made the scapegoat for something they have not done . . . even though some of both groups have at times aided the cause by their own ignorance."*

The author of *The Cosmic Conspiracy* believes there is sufficient evidence to conclude that the Illuminati used Zionism (the desire of the Jews to return and establish a refounded nation) to promote their own goals. Mr. Deyo believes it was actually the Illuminati who wrote the protocols, and many believe that Franklin, Adams, and Jefferson were likewise manipulated, at least until John Adams became alerted. In any event, as reported on page 24 of the book *The Cult of the All-Seeing Eye,* according to the Journals of Congress, 1776, Vol. 1, pages 248 and 397, Thomas Jefferson and John Adams (Masons) and Benjamin Franklin (a Rosicrucian) were appointed by the Continental Congress on July 4, 1776 to prepare a seal for the "United States of America."

Keeping in mind that this date was still 13 years before John Adams became concerned about the conspiracy, the Great Seal of the new republic was an Illuminati masterpiece. The pyramid with 13 levels ties in with the 13 colonies, but the association is with ancient Egyptian and Babylonian mysticism. The eye above the pyramid has been construed to be the "all-seeing eye" of God, but this is not what the words on the seal indicate. The words in Latin, *Anniut Coeptis – Novus Ordo Seclorum,* mean the opposit – "Announcing the Birth of a New Secular Order."

On the reverse side of the seal is the eagle, the symbol of the new nation. The eagle's shield has 13 vertical stripes, indicating the 13 states, with 12 horizontal stripes, the number of perfect government. The eagle holds an olive branch with 13 leaves and 13 olives in one claw, and 13 arrows in another claw. The meaning of this is that the United States is for peace, but is always armed for defense. The words over the eagle, *E Pluribus Unum,* mean "out of many, one." As idealistic as the motto is, it is still Babylonish in concept. Nimrod of Babel resisted God in the division of mankind into races, languages, and nations. Babylon, under Nebuchadnezzar, attempted to forge mankind back into a single race under one empire. The United States has succeeded to a limited degree in bringing all races together to forge one nation.

Some theologians, such as E. Frank Logsdon, former pastor of Moody Church in Chicago, believe that our country is the "last Babylon" mentioned in the book of Revelation. The re-forming of all nations, races, and languages into a world order under a common leader is the goal of the Illuminati society. It appears that Weishaupt, and the other Illuminists of that day, had designs to use America to bring their goals to fruition. It appears that it was only by the intervention of God, and the awareness of some of the early Founding Fathers, that this goal was thwarted.

The Illuminati emblem, the "all-seeing eye," continues to be associated with organizations and movements throughout the world that are working for a one-world, godless and secular order. Within the meditation room of the United Nations, there is an object that demands the sole attention of all who enter. Opposite the altar is a bold cubist painting. While at first glance the painting may appear to be a confusion of conflicting lines and colors, clearly outlined in the center is the round "all-seeing eye" of the Illuminati, in the middle of a pyramid. The main symbol, identified with UN higher goals, clearly relates to the ideals of Weishaupt and all Illuminists since Nimrod. Like Nimrod, the Illuminists are hunters of souls, to build a world socialistic order that deifies man and rejects Jesus Christ. Whether we call them Satanists, Communists, world humanists, or the Illuminati, they are in evidence today, and multiplying rapidly.

The motion picture *Being There,* starring Peter Sellers, was released for public view in early 1980. The movie inself is a sick comedy on contemporary American society and the political concept of government. One of the main characters in the plot is a millionaire economist and political kingmaker. On one wall of his home is clearly evident the Illuminati eye. In the course of the story this super-rich economist dies, and he is buried in a monument the shape of a pyramid with the same Illuminati emblem on top.

In one sense, the names "Illuminati" and "Satan" mean the same. In Isaiah 14:12 and other Scriptures, Lucifer is described as the "bright and shining one," or the "light bearer." This was his title before he fell. The apostle Paul wrote in II Cor. 11:14: *"And no marvel; for Satan himself is transformed into an angel of light."* The goals of Satan and of the Illuminati have always been the same: the destruction of Christianity and the institution of a world government dedicated to Satanism.

The Satanic Conspiracy

Governments are ordained by God. The apostle Paul stated this divine precept in Romans 13:1-3: *"Let every soul be subject unto the higher powers. For there is no power but of God: the powers that be are ordained of God. Whosoever therefore resisteth the power, resisteth the ordinance of God: and they that resist shall receive to themselves damnation. For rulers are not a terror to good works, but to the evil . . . "*

In this Scripture, Paul is not defending each and every king or governmental official in the world. The proposition is that God ordained nations and governments so that men might be protected from criminals and be given an opportunity to hear the truth of God proclaimed. Anyone who attempts to destroy the national structure of the world by tearing down governments for the purpose of creating an anti-God order like the one before the Flood is in rebellion against God's plan and purpose. For this reason, God continues to intervene when Satan's efforts to bring in his own kingdom on Earth give evidence of success. At times God allows despots to rule over those who have departed from His ordinances for human government. Daniel 4:17 says: *"This matter is by the decree of the watchers, and the demand by the word of the holy ones: to the intent that the living may know that the most High ruleth in the kingdom of men, and giveth it to whomsoever he will, and setteth up over it the basest of men."*

Of Lucifer, who after his initial rebellion against God became Satan, we read in Isaiah 14:12-17: *"How art thou fallen from heaven, O Lucifer, son of the morning! how art thou cut down to the ground, which didst weaken the nations! For thou hast said in thine heart, I will ascend into heaven, I will exalt my throne above the stars of God: I will sit also upon the mount of the congregation, in the sides of the north: I will ascend above the heights of the clouds; I will be like the most High. Yet thou shalt be brought down to hell, to the sides of the pit. They that see thee shall narrowly look upon thee, and consider thee, saying, Is this the man that made the earth to tremble, that did shake kingdoms; That made the world a wilderness, and destroyed the cities thereof . . . ?"*

It is Satan's purpose to weaken nations, and he is doing this today mainly through the international Communist conspiracy, an outgrowth of the Illuminati movement. *Illuminati* means "the light bearers," and *Webster's New Twentieth Century Dictionary, Unabridged,* gives the following definition of Lucifer: *"Light-bringing,* lucis, *light, and* fer, *to bear. Satan, especially as the leader of the revolt of the angels before his fall."*

On page 66 of *The Cosmic Conspiracy,* the six main goals that Adam

Weishaupt listed as primary objectives of the Illuminati through world revolutions and wars are enumerated:

1. Abolition of ordered or nationalistic governments in the form of monarchies.
2. Abolition of private property.
3. Abolition of inheritance rights.
4. Abolition of patriotism to national causes.
5. Abolition of social order in families, sexual laws, and moral codes.
6. Abolition of all religious disciplines based on faith in God as opposed to faith in nature, man and reason.

According to information provided by the Cinema Educational Guild of California, at about the time of the American Civil War, a general by the name of Albert Pike was recruited by the Illuminati, and he became the head of the organization. Pike was fascinated by the idea of a world government. Between 1859 and 1871, Pike augmented Illuminati goals with a definite timetable. Pike worked out a formulated plan for various revolutions and three world wars to overthrow existing government. He did most of his work at his home in Little Rock, Arkansas, and set up three supreme councils, located in Charleston, South Carolina; Rome, Italy; and Berlin, Germany. These councils controlled 23 other subordinate groups throughout the world. Pike's plan was relatively simple. It called for Communism, political Zionism, and Fascism to foment three global wars and at least two major revolutions. The First World War was to enable Communism to destroy the Czarist government of Russia, and replace it with militant atheism.

According to this plan credited to Pike, the governments of Great Britain and Germany were to be manipulated in order to start a world war. After the war, Communism would then be in a position to destroy other governments and weaken religions. World War II was to be fomented by using Fascism against Zionism. Hitler was financed by the Krups, the Warburgs, and the Rothschilds. The slaughter of the Jews by Fascism would be necessary to bring other nations against Germany and spread the conflict to other continents. The Second World War was to destroy Fascism and increase the power of Zionism, so that Israel would be refounded as a nation in Palestine. During this second world conflict, Communism would become equal in strength to united Christendom. When it reached that point, it was to be held in check and used when it was needed in the final cataclysm.

This reported Pike blueprint states that World War III would be instigated by using the controversy between Judaism and the Moslem world. The Zionists and the Moslems would supposedly destroy each other, bringing the rest of the world into this final conflict, Armageddon. In the aftermath, there would be complete social, political, and economic chaos.

Pike reportedly revealed his plan to another primary Illuminati agent, Mazzini, an Italian revolutionary, on August 15, 1871. After the Third World War, the world would then be ready to accept a world government. This was set up and administered by a supreme dictator appointed by the Illuminati. In the words of Pike's own letter to Mazzini, now catalogued in the British Museum in London, England, he said: *"We shall unleash the Nihilists and the atheists in a great social cataclysm which will show clearly to all nations, in all its horror, the effect of absolute atheism, the origin of savagery and of most bloody turmoil. Then everywhere, the people forced to defend themselves against the world minority of revolutionaries, will exterminate the destroyers of civilzation, and the multitudes disillusioned with Christianity whose deistic spirits will be from that moment on without direction and leadership, and anxious for an ideal but without knowledge where to send its adoration, will receive the true light through the universal manifestation that will result from a general reactionary movement that will follow the destruction of Christianity and atheism, both conquered and exterminated at the same time."*

The trail of the Illuminati is clearly traced in accepted historical records, such as *The Encyclopaedia Britannica,* through the Bavarian Revolution, the American Revolution, and the French Revolution. Thereafter, information is pieced together by letters, personal records, and political and anti-religious movements that fit into the pattern of the established conspiracy. That there is a satanic conspiracy in operation that coincides with the goals of the Illuminati is beyond question.

THE SATANIC CONSPIRACY

The account of Lucifer being cast down from Heaven to the Earth in Isaiah 14 is given from a prophetic viewpoint. Lucifer, the original revolutionary, planned to take over the Kingdom of God. We read in the Bible of war in Heaven. But at some time in the future, Lucifer, who became Satan will be cut down to the Earth. We read of this coming event in Revelation 12:12: *"Therefore rejoice, ye heavens, and ye that dwell in them. Woe to the inhabiters of the earth and of the sea! for the devil is come down unto you, having great wrath, because he knoweth that he hath but a short time."*

Jesus indicated in Matthew 24:6,7 that at the end of the age, when Satan would try to set up his kingdom on Earth, there would be wars and rumours of wars; nation would rise against nation, and kingdom against kingdom. This prophecy foreshadows revolutions and world wars to weaken the nations. Part of this satanic plan, according to Ezekiel 38 and 39, would be the rise of Communism, a mighty anti-God power in Russia. Then, according to Ezekiel, Russia would align with four Moslem nations and invade the refounded nation of Israel. Also, according to the 11th chapter of Daniel, and other prophecies in Revelation, the armies of all nations will become involved in the Middle East. It will be in those days that Satan will set up a world governmental system, and appoint his own ruler over it. This world dictator is called "the Beast," or the Antichrist. Under his administration, which will govern all the Earth, everyone in the world will be commanded to worship Satan as the supreme God of the universe.

We read of the establishment of Lucifer's kingdom on Earth in Revelation 13:4-8: *"And they worshipped the dragon which gave power unto the beast: and they worshipped the beast, saying, Who is like unto the beast; who is able to make war with him? And there was given unto him a mouth speaking great things and blasphemies; and power was given unto him to continue forty and two months. And he opened his mouth in blasphemy against God, to blaspheme his name, and his tabernacle, and them that dwell in heaven. And it was given unto him to make war with the saints, and to overcome them: and power was given him over all kindreds, and tongues, and nations. And all that dwell upon the earth shall worship him, whose names are not written in the book of life of the Lamb slain from the foundation of the world."*

It will be toward the end of the brief reign of this satanic world dictator that the armies of all nations will be gathered into the Middle East to prevent the return of Jesus Christ. We read from Zechariah 14:1-4: *"Behold, the day of the Lord cometh . . . I will gather all nations against Jerusalem to battle . . . Then shall the Lord go forth, and fight against those nations . . . And his feet shall stand in that day upon the mount of Olives, which is before Jerusalem on the east . . . "*

A more detailed description of the return of Jesus Christ with the armies of Heaven to destroy Satan's dictator, along with the armies of the world, is given in Revelation 19 and Revelation 16:11-14. The downfall of the entire satanic conspiracy is also described in II Thess. 2:7-9: *"For the mystery of iniquity doth already work: only he who now letteth will let, until he be taken out of the way. And then shall that Wicked be revealed, whom the Lord shall consume with the spirit of his mouth, and shall destroy with the brightness of his coming: Even him, whose coming is after the working of Satan with all power and signs and lying wonders."*

The only thing that is preventing the establishment of Satan's government over all nations is the Holy Spirit, who is witnessing to the world today, through Christians, about Jesus Christ and His power to save. Our understanding of the promise of God recorded in I Thess. 4:13-18 is that Christians will be taken out of the world before the time of great tribulation spoken of by Jesus in Matthew 24:21. Then Satan's world government, under the Antichrist, will be instituted upon Earth. There is indeed a Luciferian conspiracy, and it is described in great detail in the Bible. There is an Illuminati, because Satan works through his angels and representatives in the world. Whether this conspiracy is among the same people who followed Weishaupt, and their co-conspirators in the 19th and 20th centuries, is a matter of opinion. Nevertheless, we point out that their goals and methods of operation exactly parallel the satanic conspiracy so carefully and thoroughly described in prophetic Scriptures in the Bible. The Illuminati, the so-called light-bearers, will be defeated only by the brightness of Jesus Christ, the Light of the World, when He comes again.

THE FRENCH REVOLUTION

It is generally conceded that the French Revolution was a part of the Illuminati plot to rid the world of religion and inaugurate internal strife and revolution within the nations. This fact is alluded to in *The Encyclopaedia Britannica* and is fully documented by quotations from papers and records in *The French Revolution.* John Adams and others were alert to the Illuminati plot to take over the American Revolution and institute a bloody purge of the religious orders, churches, and Christians in general. This was not true of the French Revolution. Documented quotations and records in *The French Revolution* by Nesta H. Webster refer to mass slaughters at the guillotine, where ditches had to be dug to carry off the blood. Beheading is traditionally a method of execution preferred by Satan worshippers, because it is supposed to prevent a resurrection. Therefore, it seems no coincidence that the guillotine, used in the French Revolution, will again be used to kill those who do not worship Satan in the Great Tribulation.

This truth is prophetically recorded in Revelation 20:4: *"I saw the souls of them that were beheaded for the witness of Jesus, and for the word of God, and which had not worshipped the beast, neither his image, neither had received his mark upon their foreheads, or in their hands; and they lived and reigned with Christ a thousand years."*

THE RUSSIAN REVOLUTION

There is some evidence that Karl Marx was a convert of Weishaupt. Karl Heinrich Marx was a Jew. His own father thought his son to be demon possessed. From Marxism came Communism, and evidence indicates that Lenin and Trotsky were chosen to succeed Mazzini and Pike. These anti-God revolutionaries took over the Bolshevik Revolution in Russia.

It was on May 1, 1776, that Weishaupt founded the European branch of the Luciferian conspiracy under the name of the "Illuminati." May 1 has been established as the worldwide holiday of Communism. This is the day that Communist powers bring out their military weapons to threaten the Christian world with extermination.

Beyond controversy, there is a satanic conspiracy operating in the world today. Whether we call it Luciferianism, Illuminism, The New Age, Communism, or some other name, the mystery of iniquity will one day come to the full.

We leave the reader with the following advice: *"Finally, my brethren, be strong in the Lord, and in the power of his might. Put on the whole armour of God, that ye may be able to stand against the wiles of the devil. For we wrestle not against flesh and blood, but against principalities, against powers, against the rulers of the darkness of this world, against spiritual wickedness in high places. Wherefore take unto you the whole armour of God, that ye may be able to withstand in the evil day, and having done all, to stand"* (Ephesians 6:10-13).

Lucis Trust

Throughout the age-old spectrum of occult movements and organizations there has been one common emblem and name by which they have been identified. This one common denominator is the sign of the "All-seeing Eye," and the name "The Order of the Illuminati."

Throughout the history of mankind, dating back before the Flood, the existence of "illumined ones," the followers of Lucifer (the bright and shining one), can be traced. Their goal has never varied: the bringing of all nations into one common political and religious brotherhood to worship Lucifer. The changing of the agents of darkness into angels of light (II Cor. 11:14) has always been their chief mode of operation.

On May 1, 1776, Adam Weishaupt, a professor at Ingolstadt University, revived the master occult organization to become a catalyst for a great one-world push. The organization was named "The Order of the Illuminati," and agents from the Illuminati soon began infiltrating the churches. Adam Weishaupt wrote: *"These good folk swell our numbers and fill our moneybox. Set yourselves to work; these gentlemen must be made to nibble the bait. But this sort of people must always be made to believe that the grade they have reached is the last . . . The most wonderful thing of all is that the distinguished Lutheran and Calvinist theologians who belong to our Order really believe that they see in it the true and genuine sense of the Christian religion! O, mortal man, is there anything that you cannot be made to believe?"*

As we have previously mentioned, the Illuminati proceeded to work through the Masons. There is also considerable evidence that the "Illumined Ones" have also established subsidiary organizations; or at least, these organizations parallel Illuminati goals.

Recently we wrote the Lucis Trust at 866 United Nations Plaza, Suite 566-7, New York, NY, 10017. We requested information on the Illuminati, and they obligingly forwarded to us some of their own literature, indicating to us at least that both were the same. *Lucis* and *Illuminati* mean the same. Both words come from Lucifer, which means "light-bringing, or light-bearer." According to *Webster's New Twentieth Century Dictionary*, *Lucifer* and *Lucis* mean the same thing: *"Light-bringing, to bear light. Satan, especially as the leader of the revolt of the angels before his fall."*

The Lucis Trust was incorporated in 1922 under its present name. According to information that is available to us, prior to that time it was known as the Lucifer Trust. The reason for changing the name to another form is obvious. In the literature forwarded to us by Lucis Trust is a leaflet telling something about its history; however, no mention is made of its existence prior to 1922. Under the heading "Creation and Operation" we read the following:

"The Lucis Trust was incorporated in the United States in 1922. It is officially recognized by the Federal Government and by various State Governments as tax-exempt. The Lucis Trust is not endowed. It is a non-profit world service organization receiving and using monies to promote activities concerned with the establishment of right human relations and world cooperation and sharing. The Lucis Trust is registered in Great Britain, in Holland and in Germany. It has bank accounts or financial agents in many other countries, including Geneva, Switzerland, where the European headquarters of the work is established. The financial and legal affairs of the Lucis Trust are controlled by an international Board of Trustees, aided by additional Trustees and elected Officers and members in different countries. Enough men of goodwill working to create the new world order of brotherhood, cooperation, and right relationship, can defeat the forces of materialism and liberate a sense of shared responsibility for human welfare within the hearts and minds of men."

Nothing is said in the brochure about how the financial agents of Lucis Trust in the nations in which they operate receive contributions, or monies, or who their donors are. The basic purpose of the Lucis Trust, according to its own statements, is to establish a new world order of "brotherhood." The different mission avenues used by Lucis Trust are listed in the main pamphlet that sets forth their purposes: *"Activities: The activities of the Lucis Trust include the worldwide financial support of the Arcane School, the Lucis Publishing Companies, World Goodwill, Triangles, Lucis Trust Libraries and Radio Lucis."*

The word *arcane* means "mystical, or of the occult," yet the Lucis Trust professes to believe in God. The teachings of the organization are translated into over 50 languages and the message finds its way into most nations by literature and radio, according to their claims.

The common "prayer" of the Lucis Trust is called "The Great Invocation":
"From the point of Light within the Mind of God Let light stream forth into the minds of Men Let Light descend on Earth. From the point of Love within the Heart of God Let love stream forth into the hearts of men. May Christ return to Earth. From the centre where the will of God is known Let purpose guide the little wills of men — The purpose which the Masters know and serve. From the centre which we call the race of men Let the plan of love and light work out. And may it seal the door where evil dwells. Let light and Love and Power restore the Plan on Earth."

Once again it should be noted how light, or the illumination of the minds of men, is stressed. The Lucis Trust claims to believe in the Second Coming of Christ, but a close examination of their material reveals they believe and teach witchcraft, and deny that Jesus is actually the Christ who is coming back. From their brochure listing 24 Books of Esoteric Philosophy we read: *"A Treatise on White Magic — This book contains the fifteen rules for Magic . . . the White Magician, becoming manifest through its own inherent 'magical' powers. Man is essentially and inherently divine. The soul is the means whereby mankind evolves a consciousness of divinity, redeems gross matter and liberates the pure flame of spirit from the limitation of form."*

On the Second Coming Of Christ, the same brochure states: *"The Reappearance of the Christ: Many religions today expect the coming of an Avator or Saviour. The second coming of Christ, as the world Teacher for the age of Aquarius, is presented in this book as an imminent event, logical and practical in the continuity of divine revelation through the ages. The Christ belongs to all mankind; he can be known and understood as 'the same great Identity in all the world religions.' "*

In other words, Lucis Trust proposes that the Christ of Christians is the same as the Christ of the Moslems, the Hindus, the Buddhists, etc. One of the books distrubited by Lucis Trust is titled *Esoteric Astrology*, and the advertisement reads: *"The science of esoteric astrology is said to be the basic occult science of the future. Astrology is described in this book as 'the science of relationships', a science which deals with those conditioning energies and forces which play through and upon the whole field of space and all that is found within it."*

How much credit the Lucis Trust can claim for the great revival in occult activities and astrology in these last days is not known, but it may be considerable. A friend and listener of The Southwest Radio Church who resides on the West Coast attended a meeting sponsored by the Lucis Trust. She wrote an article based on what was said. This listener does not want her name revealed. We quote from her article just as it was forwarded to us:

Values To Choose By

"Mary Bailey has been touring the United States and Canada ... She represents the Arcane School (occultism), the Lucis Publishing companies (formerly LUCIFER), and the alleged world service activities known as Triangles and World Goodwill.

"It is more than a little curious how closely the goals of Lucis Trust resemble the radically changing goals of church, state, and religion, both here and abroad. Promising 'a new and better way of life for all men everywhere in the world' through 'practical techniques in operation today' toward the 'fulfillment of the divine plan for humanity,' the Lucis Trust is accelerating smoothly towards its pseudo-religious objective of global 'unity' – that prophetic condition in which all political, state, and spiritual powers are identical. Students of the Arcane School and all the multi-faceted approaches of the esoteric philosophy, view this condition as heralding the New Age Consciousness, the Golden Dawn of Humanity.

"Mrs. Bailey pointed out that, throughout the ages, the world has been given various forms of teaching and guidance, even divine intervention. She listed in this order, the following sources of said instructions: 'the Ageless Wisdom Teaching, the major world religions, Buddhism, Christianity, Mohammedanism; and each, as it has appeared, has established certain principles.'

Predictably, the Lord Jesus Christ was casually equated with 'other great teachers,' ignoring any consideration of His divinity in a subtle sea of esoteric semantics. The major portion of Mrs. Bailey's discourse concentrated upon what she considered the more dynamic cosmic principles and esoteric teachings which finally are coming to the fore-front 'to procede and condition the New Age, the Aquarian Age, into which we are now moving . . . with new energies.' She added, 'energy is going to produce its effect.'

"A few of the questions asked that evening confirmed, for the Christian, the specific identity behind the Lucis Trust.

"A young girl asked, 'Do you think we may see the second coming of Christ?'

"Mrs. Bailey replied, 'This event could occur in our time. There are three ways in which it might occur: (1) Through the awakening of the Christ-principle in the human heart, which is already beginning; (2) By the mental overshadowing of the disciples; (3) By the actual physical reappearance, when conditions are right.'

"Mrs. Bailey explained, 'It is unlikely he will be known by the name of Jesus, because . . . it is considered that the master Jesus and the Christ are, in fact, two separate identities. The Christ overshadows the master Jesus. He is not the Christ. He was used by the Christ. What name will be given Christ at his second coming, I have no idea. It is said that his work will involve WORLD-PLANNING, WORLD RECONSTRUCTION, and not necessarily confined to churches. He will work with any group that has prepared itself sufficiently. Yes, he could be an individual, or else reappear in group form. The real problem of course, would be recognition.' After explaining to a gentleman the meaning of the hierarchy of 'superhuman consciousness' who are known by various names including The Masters of Wisdom, The Lords of Compassion, and The Society of Illumined Minds who are 'more evolved than we are,' Mrs. Bailey moved to adjourn the meeting. The evening's keynote was 'Work . . . There are enough of us now, you know, to tip the scales.' "

What we reported six years ago that Mary Bailey predicted is just now making the news headlines. The connection between Mary Bailey and Alice Bailey, cheif theoretician for the New Age Movement through the 50's and 60's is that they were both married to Foster Bailey.

Winston Churchill said in 1920: *"From the days of Sparticus, to Weishaupt, to Karl Marx, to Trotsky, the worldwide conspiracy for the overthrow of civilization and for the reconstitution of society on the basis of arrested development and envious malevolence, and impossible equality has been steadily growing. It has been the mainspring of every subversive movement during the nineteenth century."*

The effort to bring forth a world messiah, the Antichrist of prophecy, by a Satanic world conspiracy can be traced back to the Garden of Eden. The founders of Lucis Trust proposed since 1918 to bring forth a world christ in 1982 or 1983. The contemporary name for this plan is called "The New Age Movement".

On April 25, 1982, major newspapers around the world carried a full-page paid advertisement which proclaimed in part:

"In Answer To Our Call For Help, As World Teacher For All Humanity, The CHRIST IS NOW HERE. How will We Recognize Him? Look for a modern man concerned with modern problems – political, economical, and social. Since July 1977, the Christ has been emerging as a spokesman for a group or community in a well-known modern country ... Throughout history, humanity's evolution has been guided by a group of enlightened men, the Masters of Wisdom ... At the center of this 'Spiritual Hierarchy' stands the World Teacher, Lord Maitreya, known by Christians as the Christ. And as Christians await the Second Coming, so the Jews await the Messiah, the Buddhists the fifth Buddha, the Moslims the Iman Madhi, and the Hindus await Krishna."

The Elijah of this christ was Benjamin Creme, and the messiah effort was made through Tara organizations, a front for the New Age Movement. When Creme's christ did not appear as promised, the main thrust of the New Age Movement, Lucifer's Trust, took up the banner. In the October 1982 edition of Reader's Digest, page 203, appeared a full-page ad displaying *The Great Invocation* of the New Age Movement under the paid sponsorship of Lucis Trust. In smaller type at the bottom of the ad Lucis Trust entreated every individual, regardless of faith, to pray The Great Invocation so that the World's saviour will come.

This catalyst spirit agency which works between religious groups and the UN through the power of the "Illumined Minds" to bring in a world government is not heralding the return of Jesus Christ, but rather, the appearing of Antichrist. All forces in the world today promoting a one-world government and a one-world religion are working for the same goal: to weaken the nations and bring them to that day mentioned in Revelation 13:4,7,8: *"And they worshipped the dragon which gave power unto the beast: and they worshipped the beast, saying, Who is like unto the beast? who is able to make war with him? ... And it was given unto him to make war with the saints, and to overcome them: and power was given him over all kindreds, and tongues, and nations. And all that dwell upon the earth shall worship him, whose names are not written in the book of life of the Lamb slain from the foundation of the world."*

Jesus warned of the last days in Matthew 24:24: *"For there shall arise false Christs, and false prophets, and shall shew great signs and wonders; insomuch that, if it were possible, they shall deceive the very elect."*

It is also well to consider I John 4:1-3:*Beloved, believe not every spirit, but try the spirits whether they are of God: because many false prophets are gone out into the world. Hereby know ye the Spirit of God: Every spirit that confesseth not that Jesus Christ is come in the flesh is not of God: and this is that spirit of antichrist, whereof ye have heard that it should come ... "*

Anyone who preaches that the Christ is coming, but denies that He is the same Jesus who went away in accordance with Acts 1:11, is by biblical definition hearlding the Antichrist.

Satanism In Government

WORLD WAR ONE

Christians are exhorted in I Timothy 2:1,2 to pray for all those in positions of authority in government: *"I exhort therefore, that, first of all, supplications, prayers, intercessions, and giving of thanks, be made for all men; For kings, and for all that are in authority; that we may lead a quiet and peaceable life in all godliness and honesty."*

According to Paul, Christians should "first of all" remember leaders in governmental administration in their prayers. The reason for this high priority given them in prayer is that men and women might come to the knowledge that Jesus Christ is Lord and Saviour. It is also God's will that His anointed King, His only begotten Son, Jesus Christ, be the Ruler of all nations (Psalm 2; Revelation 19).

After the Flood, God ordained human government in order that mankind would be divided into nations. The governments of these nations were given the authority to punish criminals and maintain order, that all flesh would not again be corrupted as it had been before the Flood. It is Satan's desire to destroy governments, corrupt all flesh, and bring the world under the authority of his own king, the Antichrist. The battle rages within the realm of kings, princes, presidents, governors, and legislators.

When Jesus Christ chose twelve apostles, He offered His own Kingdom from Heaven to Israel. Twelve is the number of government. But Satan found a weak spot in one of the apostles; it is recorded in John 13:27 that Judas was possessed by the devil, and he subsequently betrayed the Messiah. This satanic plot to kill God's anointed King resulted from Jesus' refusal to accept the devil's proposition in Matthew 4:8,9, when *"... the devil taketh him up into an exceeding high mountain, and showeth him all the kingdoms of the world, and the glory of them; And saith unto him, All these things will I give thee, if thou wilt fall down and worship me."*

Satan has made this same offer to various men down through the centuries. He made it to Nebuchadnezzar, to Alexander, to Julius Caesar, to Genghis Khan, to Napoleon, to Lenin, and to Hitler. To whoever will listen, Satan says, "I will give you anything you want, even all the kingdoms of this world, if you will fall down and worship me."

Of course, Jesus knew that the devil had never made good on this offer, nor could he. The kingdoms of this world do not belong to him (John 14:30, II Cor. 14:4, Eph. 6:12). He is only a usurper, a revolutionary in temporary possession. Even Satan's greatest dictator, the coming Antichrist, will hold dominion over the nations for only three and one-half years. But in attempting to destroy the national composition of the world and bring mankind back to a status of rebellion as before the Flood — an era in which the devil was almost successful in capturing the entire human race — wars result. War is the greatest method of mass murder ever conceived, and it is apparent from John 8:44 that the devil has been behind every war that has been fought. Concerning the last days, Jesus said that when Satan would begin to marshall his forces as referred to in Revelation 12, then " . . . *nation shall rise against nation, and kingdom against kingdom . . . "* (Matthew 24:7).

On June 28, 1914, in Sarajevo, Austria, people gathered by the thousands to see Archduke Francis Ferdinand, heir to the throne, and his wife Sophia. Suddenly a man named Gavrilo Princip, a member of a Satan worship cult known as the Black Hand, ran up to the automobile and assassinated both the archduke and his wife. Austria blamed Serbia and the next month, on July 2, 1914, declared war. In a period of three months, forty-three nations were at war with each other over the act of a Satanist. Other nations became involved, and soon this greatest conflict that had ever been known was called the First World War.

KARL MARX

The initiation of a form of government that would actually defy God did not begin with Lenin. It began with a male child born in 1818, Karl Heinrich Marx. His father was a lawyer and a Christian. Being of an upper middle-class family, young Marx attended law school at Bonn University in 1835. He subsequently transferred to the University of Berlin, where he received a Doctor of Philosophy degree in 1841. Seven years later he joined revolutionaries to overthrow the government of Germany. The revolution was not successful, and Karl Marx fled to England, where he resided until his death in 1883. His closest associate was Friedrich Engels, and together they composed the *Communist Manifesto.*

However, Karl Marx, at least in his earlier life, was not an atheist. Although born a Jew, he was reared in a Christian home, and he was baptized in the Orthodox Church. He was a faithful church member in his earlier school years. In his first work, titled "The Union of the Faithful with Christ," he expressed his faith in the atoning death of Jesus Christ. Whether Karl Marx ever accepted Christ as his own personal Saviour is debatable, and we read in James 2:19 that even devils believe in the existence of God. In any event, he was an apostate. Like Judas Iscariot and all other apostates, he evidently knew the truth but exercised his own free will to reject it. From all appearances, before Karl Marx received his degree from the university, his faith in the Lord Jesus Christ had completely reversed. A dramatic poem that Marx called *Oulanem* demonstrated the depth of his apostasy. *Oulanem* is an anagram of *Emmanuel*, which in Scripture is a name for Jesus Christ, meaning "God with us." Anagrams and backward statements of biblical truths are common in Satan worship. The satanic Black Mass consists of saying the Lord's prayer in reverse to demonstrate defiance against God. We quote a few sentences from *Oulanem*, by Karl Marx:

> *Till I go mad and my heart is utterly*
> *Changed, See this sword — the Prince of Darkness*
> *Sold it to me . . .*
> *While for us both the abyss yawns in darkness*
> *You will sink down and I shall follow laughing.*
> *Whispering in your ears, "Descend,*
> *Come with me, friend." . . .*
> *If there is something which devours,*
> *I'll leap within it, though I bring the world*
> *To ruins —*
> *The world which bulks between me and the abyss,*
> *I'll smash it to pieces with my enduring*
> *Curses.*
> *I'll throw my arms around its harsh*
> *Reality.*
> *Embracing me, the world will dumbly pass*
> *Away.*
> *And then sink down to utter nothingness,*
> *Perished, with no existence: That would be*
> *Really living.*

The rejection of Jesus Christ as God's annointed King and the denial of God Himself as Creator permeate Communist doctrine. Karl Marx avowed that the devil had sold him a plan for the world. About the time that he wrote *Oulanem*, he also wrote a letter to his Christian father, which stated in part: *"A curtain has fallen. My Holy of Holies was rent asunder and New Gods installed."* The elder Marx replied to his son's letter, *"Only if your heart remains pure and beats humanly, and if no demon will be able to alienate your heart, only then will I be happy."*

Karl Marx's father believed his son was demon possessed when he wrote the *Communist Manifesto*. Edgar Marx, the son of Karl Marx, addressed his father in a letter dated March 31, 1854, "My Dear Devil."

Rev. Richard Wurmbrand, a minister who spent many years in a Communist prison, said of Karl Marx: *"Have you ever wondered about Marx's hair style? Men usually wore beards in his time, but not beards like his, and they did not have long hair. Marx's manner of bearing himself was characteristic of the disciples of Joana Southcott, a Satanic Priestess who considered herself in contact with the demon Shiloh."* Karl Marx's closest friend, Friedrich Engels, wrote of Marx in one of his fits of anger and depression: *"He does not walk or run, he jumps on his heels and rages full of anger . . . He stretches his arms far away in the air; the wicked fist is clenched, he rages without ceasing, as if ten thousand devils would have caught him by the hair."*

The clenched fist raised toward heaven in defiance of God was a trademark of

Karl Marx. But even before Marx, Lucifer, as described in Isaiah 14:12-17, shook his fist at God and raged, "I will ascend into heaven! I will be like the most High! I will exalt my throne above the stars of God!"

Karl Marx declared that he would bring the present world system to ashes, fling his glove in the face of God, and walk over the Earth a creator. There is ample evidence that Communism, which controls approximately one-half the people of the world at the present time, was born and propagated in demon-possessed men. Communism is one of Satan's ways to destroy the national structures established by God in order to bring his own kingdom of darkness upon the Earth. He will succeed for a short period when he brings his own false messiah to power during the great Tribulation. In the meantime, Communist armies are poised to strike in the Middle East at this present hour to further extend this satanic system of government. It is no wonder that God, in looking at Russia in the last days, has said: "... *Thus saith the Lord God; Behold, I am against thee, O Gog, the chief prince of Meshech* [Moscow] *and Tubal* [Tobolsk] " (Ezekiel 38:3).

WORLD WAR TWO

World War I was described at its end as "the war to end all wars." But Jesus said there would be wars, meaning many conflicts, in the end of the age. The greatest war that mankind had ever experienced was rapidly followed by an even greater one – World War II. The agent that Satan used was a man named Adolf Hitler. A pamphlet that was distributed to young Germans, entitled, "Leaves of the White Rose," by opponents of Hitler, read in part:

"Every word out of Hitler's mouth is a lie. If he says peace, he means war, and if he calls frivolously on the name of the Almighty, he means the power of Evil, the Fallen Angel, the Devil. His mouth is the stinking throat of hell ... Certainly one has to fight against the Nazi terror state with rational weapons, but whosoever still doubts the real existence of demonical powers has not understood the metaphysical background of this war. Behind the concrete and perceptible things, behind all real and logical considerations, there is the irrational, there is the fight against the Demon, against the messenger of Anti-christ. Everywhere and at all times the demons have lurked in the dark for the hour when man becomes weak, when he arbitrarily abandons his human situation in the world order founded by God for him on freedom ... "

Hitler was an artist of sorts who peddled his paintings in watercolors to get enough money to live in a 25 cents-a-night flophouse in Vienna. There was nothing evil in this of itself, because many artists get their start this way. But it was during this period of poverty and frustration that Hitler saw the wealth of the Jews in Vienna. Regardless of the status of the Jew, whether it be affluency or degradation, God has said: *"I will bless them that bless thee, and curse him that curseth thee ... "* (Gen. 12:3). The deeper Hitler sank into poverty, the more bitter he became; and he directed his hatred toward the Jews. It was then that Satan found in young Hitler a tool he could use.

After World War I, Hitler joined the Thule Society, a satanic organization that claimed credit for more than 400 assassinations. The leader of the group, Dietrich Eckhart, boasted that he *"would prepare the vessel of the Anti-christ, the man inspired by Lucifer to conquer the world and lead the Aryan race to glory."* On his deathbed, Eckhart is reported to have said: *"Do not mourn me: I shall have influenced history more than any other German. Follow Hitler . . . ! I have initiated him into the Secret Doctrine, opened his centres of vision and given him the means to communicate with the powers."*

Practically all of Hitler's top aides — Goebbels, Himmler, and Goering, to name a few — belonged to occult groups. Willy Ley, a scientist who left Germany, warned that the Nazis were using occult powers to create a super race. During World War II, that indeed seemed to be the case; in spite of overwhelming odds, the German army seemed to be invincible.

From Matthew 12:24-26, we know that Satan has a host of demonic powers under his control. We read in Acts 8:9-11 that Satan controlled Samaria through a sorcerer named Simon. In Daniel, the fact is presented that Satan has his own servants in control of nations. It is the aim of Satan to establish his own kingdom on Earth and then prevent Jesus Christ from bringing in the Kingdom from Heaven. We read in Revelation 13:7 that one day Satan's man, the Antichrist, after the order of Adolf Hitler, will have control over all nations, races, and languages. This struggle is going on in the world at the present hour, and is leading up to the revelation of the devil's man, foretold in II Thessalonians 2:8,9: *"And then shall that Wicked be revealed, whom the Lord shall consume with the spirit of his mouth, and shall destroy with the brightness of his coming: Even him, whose coming is after the working of Satan with all power and signs and lying wonders . . . "*

Satan's Last Stand

When one nation attacks another in open combat, the war entails much more than soldiers pointing their guns at each other and pulling the triggers. Modern warfare involves the airways, the seaways, ground battles, and bombing of communication and transportation arteries, the destruction of factories, and even civilian terroristic bombing attacks.

The same applies to Satan's war against God. It is a total rebellion, employing every means at the devil's disposal. This war involves the powers of the air, rulers in government, the occult, demons, the devil's angels, apostasy in the churches, lusts of the flesh, and personal attacks on believers.

In Revelation 12:9,10, the Scripture states that the devil accuses the brethren before God day and night. In verse 12 the apostle John by revelation from Jesus Christ saw the frantic and desperate activities of Satan in the last days because of the soon return of our Lord and Saviour as God's anointed King over the Earth. As never before, Satan and his hordes are raging over the Earth, attacking everything that is of God.

ATTACK ON THE CHURCH

A massive literature campaign against the churches of this nation is underway. It is openly stated by New Age Movement proponents that the fundamental Christians who oppose the dawning of the New Age will simply disappear. A booklet published by World Goodwill, a front for Lucis Trust, titled *The New World Religion*, states in part:

"Today, slowly, the concept of a world religion and the need for its emergence are widely desired and worked for. The fusion of faiths is now a field of discussion. Workers in the field of religion will formulate the universal platform of the new world religion. This group is, in a pronounced sense, a channel for the activities of the Christ, the world Teacher. The platform of the new world religion will by built by many groups, working under the inspiration of the Christ.

"Churchmen need to remember that the human spirit is greater than all the churches and greater than their teaching. In the long run, that human spirit will defeat them and proceed triumphantly into the Kingdom of God, leaving them far behind unless they enter as a humble part of the mass of men. Nothing under heaven can arrest the progress of the human soul on its long pilgrimage from darkness to light, from the unreal to the real, from death to immortality and from ignorance to wisdom. If the great organized religious groups of churches in every land, and composing all faiths do not offer spiritual guidance and help,

humanity will find another way. Nothing can keep the spirit of man from God.

"God works in many ways, through many faiths and religious agencies; this is one reason for the elimination of non-essential doctrines. By the emphasizing of the essential doctrines and in their union will the fullness of truth be revealed. This, the new world religion will do and its implementation will proceed apace, after the reappearance of the Christ."

No where in this booklet, or in any New Age literature, is the Christ called Jesus. In fact, they say that Jesus is not the Christ, but that He is one of the Masters. The Christ the New Age is proposing is Antichrist.

ATTACK AGAINST GOVERNMENT

God ordained human government. Paul wrote of government as recorded in Romans 13:1: *"Let every soul be subject unto the higher powers. For there is no power but of God: the powers that be are ordained of God."*

God established nations to be ruled by governments so that the entire world would not be corrupted by Satan as it was before the Flood: *"God that made the world . . . hath made of one blood all nations of men for to dwell on all the face of the earth, and hath determined the times before appointed, and the bounds of their habitation; That they should seek the Lord, if haply they might feel after him . . . "* (Acts 17:24,26,27).

The structuring of mankind into nations is a bulwark against Satan's plan to take over Earth as part of his kingdom forever. Of course, the devil will be successful for a brief period of three and one-half years, when all races and peoples and languages will worship the Antichrist as their God (Rev. 13:8). But in these last days there have been many attempts to bring all nations into a one-world dictatorial order. The movement began with the League of Nations. Although the United States did not join the League of Nations, out of this organization came the Council on Foreign Relations, the United Nations, the Trilateral Commission, and many other one-world governments.

International Communism is another threat to the individual identity of nations. It is the goal of Communism to bring all races and languages into a socialistic order in which one governing body would rule over the entire world for what "it" would determine was the common good. Whether there is a one-world system under Communism, a one-world order under the United Nations, or a one-world government under any other sponsorship, Satan will still win as far as his goal is concerned to bring all nations to war against God's anointed King. This he will do, as described in Revelation 19, to try to prevent the return of Jesus Christ.

SATAN'S NUMBER

In 1982 we invited Constance Cumbey, a lawyer from Detroit, Michigan who has devoted herself to exposing the New Age Movement as Satan's attempt to bring in his own counterfeit kingdom, to present a series of messages on this subject over our radio ministry. We share with you just one of the letters we received in response to her timely warning:

"I am writing in regards to the interviews your church had with Constance Cumbey a few months ago. I received copies of the tapes from a friend of mine a week ago. I am truly amazed at her message – in fact it's difficult to believe it. Yet, I sense it really is true.

"One of the reasons why I sense Mrs. Cumbey's message is true is because I have been witnessing some of those 'New Age Movement' activities in the company where I work. The friend who gave me the tapes, as well as myself, work at Northwestern Bell Telephone Company in Minnesota. We are both in management positions. A few weeks ago, my friend (a Christian) went to a seminar which our company purchased from Louis Tice of Pacific Institute. The name of the seminar is 'New Age Thinking.' At that time, he had never heard of the New Age Movement; neither had I. Through out the three day seminar, he said he was greatly troubled by many things that were being said. There seemed to be a strong flavor of 'mind control' techniques being taught.

"A week or so after finishing the seminar, some friends of his gave him the Cumbey tapes. Very quickly the 'light' came on.

"Because we have shared in the past of the many ways that our company has been supporting (unknowingly) all types of humanism movements, he called me to let me know about the content of the seminar and of the Cumbey tapes. He then sent me the tapes. After listening to the tapes, I began to understand why some other things I had read (company literature) had made me uncomfortable. For example, consider the following:

"This past summer A.T.& T. published a report to all management people in the Bell System addressing a new service soon to be offered. It's called Cellular Telephone Service. In essence it has the capability to equip each individual in our country with a type of transmitter to instantly communicate with anyone else, and more importantly, to communicate with computers. In fact, the computers are referred to as 'omnipresent data banks.' How about that! Could it be the reincarnation of the Tree of Knowledge? Another amazing thing about this is the channel requirements. There has been 30 cities selected to locate the 'control centers.' At each control center, there needed to be a specific number of microwave channels, carefully designed to provide universal service to all people. A few months ago, the FCC approved the number of channels for each center – 666! I was troubled when I read this, now I know why.

"With a communication service marked as '666,' and a seminar on New Age Thinking, both being unveiled within the past few months, I find Mrs. Cumbey's message extremely enlightening. The question is, 'What do I do now?' "

ATTACK AGAINST THE UNSAVED WORLD

Besides attacks against governments, churches, and families, Satan is also working frantically on the lower levels, at the individual level. Man was created in the image of God for a kingdom of eternal righteousness for Jesus Christ (Col. 1:12-16). It is the devil's plan to incorporate the present unsaved generation into his own kingdom of darkness through demonic possession and control. This fact is set forth in II Thess. 2:7-12.

Dr. Kurt Koch in his book *The Devil's Alphabet* lists 172 cases of demon possession that he had personally encountered. John P. Newport in his book *Demons, Demons, Demons*, writes: *"Is this a demonic age? It is in the sense that there appears to be a struggle – both cosmic and historical – moving toward a crescendo – between the forces of God and the forces of the satanic powers ... Reports of demonic influence and possession flow in from dozens of sources. Foreign mission boards in the United States continue to receive reports of such demonic activity. An exhaustive study of demon possession in China by J.L. Nevius is based on dozens of questionairres sent to missionaries and Chinese Christians before the Communist take-over ... In recent years, home mission boards report a high incidence of demon possession in the United States ... Christian workers in California state that they have had to study demon possession in order to minister to the 'hip' culture. They report that hundreds of California young people are demonized. Drugs and occult practices, such as black magic, seances, and fortune telling have evidently been a 'springboard' for the increase of interest in demon possession."*

Witchcraft, astrology, drugs, alcohol, and pornography are all wiles of the devil to corrupt the flesh of mankind in these days. Almost every edition of our local paper reports news of occult activities.

Today, Satan is marshalling his forces for the last great effort to exalt his throne above God and add the Earth to his dominion of evil. When the devil thinks he has gained sufficient strength to challenge the power of God, Paul writes in II Thess. 2:8,9: *"And then shall that Wicked be revealed, whom the Lord shall consume with the spirit of his mouth, and shall destroy with the brightness of his coming: Even him, whose coming is after the working of Satan with all power and signs and lying wonders."*

Satan will be given seven years to bring in his kingdom upon Earth, but then Jesus will return with the armies of Heaven to put an end to this period, the greatest tribulation the world has ever known, as told in Revelation 19:20–20:3 *"And the beast was taken, and with him the false prophet that wrought miracles before him, with which he deceived them that had received the mark of the beast, and them that worshipped his image. These both were cast alive into a lake of fire burning with brimstone. And the remnant were slain with the sword of him that sat upon the horse, which sword proceeded out of his mouth: and all the fowls were filled with their flesh. And I saw an angel come down from heaven, having the key of the bottomless pit and a great chain in his hand. And he laid hold of the dragon, that old serpent, which is the Devil, and Satan, and bound him a thousand years, And cast him into the bottomless pit, and shut him up, and set a seal upon him, that he should deceive the nations no more, till the thousand years should be fulfilled: and after that he must be loosed a little season."*

Satan will be bound for a thousand years. At this time the sin curse will be restrained and mankind will enjoy a period of peace and prosperity. Then, for a little while, he will be freed to work again on Earth. After that "little season," his final doom will come.

Today, as the times draw to a close, Satan is wreaking increasing havoc in every sphere of life. The times are dark, and the world without the Light of God seems without hope. But Christians have a Blessed Hope, and know that the same Jesus who was crucified and rose again will return at the end of the age and save us from Earth's darkest hour. *"For God hath not appointed us to wrath, but to obtain salvation by our Lord Jesus Christ, Who died for us, that, whether we wake or sleep, we should live together with him"* (I Thess. 5:9,10). Christians know that the flourishing of evil is but a sign of their Lord's imminent return.

Christ has told us: *"And when these things begin to come to pass, then look up, and lift up your heads; for your redemption draweth nigh"* (Luke 21:28). As evil grows and the days shrink, Christians should be examining their lives and looking up, lifting up their heads praying the last prayer in the Bible, from Revelation 22:20: *"Even so, come, Lord Jesus."*